THE EVERYBODY-BRING-A-DISH COOKBOOK

THE EVERYBODY-BRING-A-DISH COOKBOOK

Menus and Recipes for an International Eat-In

THEODORA ZAVIN

WITH

Jane Anton

Marion Brown

Elizabeth Granville

Phyllis Shulman

Patricia Quinn Stuart

QUADRANGLE / *The New York Times Book Co.*

Library of Congress Catalog Card Number: 72-85165

International Standard Book Number: 0-8129-0432-X

For Ben

BECAUSE I'VE NEVER BEEN ABLE TO COUNT

ACKNOWLEDGMENTS

A deep bow to the members of the Eat In, Jane and Ronald Anton, Marion and Robert Brown, Elizabeth and Irwin Granville, Phyllis and Alan Shulman, Patricia and Harvey Stuart and Benjamin Zavin, with whom it has been a pleasure to cook and to dine.

And another to the members of the California branch who so generously contributed their recipes: Leatrice and Herbert Eiseman, Joan and Charles Fox, Norman and Elinor Gimbel and Ilene and Richard Landy.

My thanks also to Naomi Benowitz who proved that the world's best executive secretary could tackle even so unaccustomed a job as a cookbook manuscript and do it with her usual grace and efficiency.

The warmest thanks of all to Elizabeth Granville who did the line drawings, read the manuscript, retested recipes (with the aid of her daughter Alexandra, the youngest gourmet cook I know) and provided the push without which this might never have emerged from the file drawer.

CONTENTS

THE EVERYBODY-BRING-A-DISH COOKBOOK

INTRODUCTION

Once upon a time there were five women who liked to cook who, fortunately, were married to five men who liked to eat. This phenomenon is rarer than you might think, since in my lexicon no man fits this description whose idea of a good meal revolves around steak, baked potato and any-thing-for-dessert-as-long-as-it's-chocolate-cake-but-I-don't-mind-apple-pie-once-in-a-while. My definition of a man who enjoys food is one who is sufficiently enthusiastic about experimentation to accept cheerfully the fact that every once in a while some new recipe is going to prove to be better to read than to eat and the family is going to end up raiding the refrigerator that night.

At any rate, our five couples formed a little club which, for lack of a better name, has become known as "The Eat-In." (Jane and Ron Anton, who were original members, moved to California and started a West Coast branch, known as S.T.U.F.F.—Society to Unify Food Freaks.) The idea is very simple. One Saturday night each month we meet at the home of a member couple for a dinner prepared in the style of a particular country. The country is either chosen at random from a pile of index cards, each of which bears the name of a country, or the hostess is allowed to choose the country if she wishes. Each member is responsi-ble for one course of the dinner. Thus, our card for the Hawaiian dinner read as follows:

1

Introduction

Hawaii

Hostess: Jane Anton 8/29/73
Appetizer or Soup: Marion Brown
Main Course: Jane Anton
Vegetable or Salad: Pat Stuart
Bread and Wine: Thea Zavin
Dessert: Elizabeth Granville

The hostess, who does the main course, advises the others in advance what it will be. The others swap information as each decides on her dish. This is about all the coordination you really need just to make sure that if the main course is fish you don't include a fish appetizer as well.

You can, if space permits, have six member couples. In that case the hostess would do nothing other than set the table, provide coffee and wash up. This has its advantages. We restricted our group to five couples because most of us live in Manhattan apartments with dining areas which won't seat twelve comfortably.

While our Eat-In happens to have five married couples, there is much to be said for a group comprised of five single people—men and/or women who enjoy cooking—each of whom is privileged to invite a guest for dinner. Maybe with the advent of Women's Lib young women no longer have trouble in taking the initiative in asking attractive men for dates, but the Eat-In is a great way to expand one's social horizons. The man who turns down this kind of invitation either doesn't like people or doesn't like food and even one of these characteristics should disqualify him as a person worth cultivating.

2

This book grew out of our Eat-In. You can use it as a source book for an Eat-In group of your own. You will save the many hours of research we expended culling cookbooks and picking the brains and recipe collections of our friends, neighbors and fellow workers with mixed ethnic backgrounds.

All of these recipes are designed to feed ten people. If you're a rugged individualist, you can make yourself the neighborhood's most admired hostess by specializing in exotic dinner parties. Obviously, you can cut them down proportionately if you want to prepare dinner for a smaller group. When each person is responsible for only one dish, she can afford to take time and trouble with it, and every course can be more special than if a single cook has to balance complicated courses with simple ones in order to maintain her sanity.

Our group lives surrounded by great restaurants, and we have traveled enough to have enjoyed the treasures of La Reserve at Beaulieu, The White Tower in London, Los Caracoles in Barcelona and similar delightful establishments which lighten the weight of your traveler's checks while not, unfortunately, performing the same service for your person. But our recommendation is that you do your globe-trotting right at home at your own dinner table. For overall excitement, the Eat-In gets our vote.

A few of the menus require ingredients which may be unavailable at your regular shopping centers. Where there are specialized ingredients needed (as with the Chinese or Indian dinners, for example) you will find at the end of the introduction to the chapter. Before you decide to order by mail, however, check your local sources if you live in a medium or large city. The food editor of your local newspaper or your radio or television station may be able to guide you to shops you never dreamed existed in your area.

While this is primarily a gastronomic journey around the world, we did on two occasions travel in time as well. Our eighteenth-century American dinner is particularly appropriate for a July 4th Eat-In. Because the cooking of early New England has remained part of our lives in terms of the traditional Thanksgiving dinner, we turned to Colonial Virginia for our United States stopover. Our English dinner, held on New Year's Eve, was a Dickens Christmas dinner with the Cratchits' dinner menu enhanced by Charles Dickens' own recipe for Christmas punch—and if that doesn't make you merry, you're in line for a visit from Jacob Marley.

You won't find the countries arranged either in alphabetical order or in any significant geographical sequence. They are very much in the order in which we had our dinners—designed to give contrast between one month's dinner and the next.

Just one word on the subject of authenticity. If you're familiar with the cuisine of any of the countries we've toured in this book, you'll recognize that we have sometimes blithely mixed regions of a country in a single dinner. If you were asked, for example, to prepare an American meal for a foreign visitor, would you choose New England or New Orleans cuisine? Southwest barbecue or Southeast ham with redeye gravy? While purists may object to our mingling regional specialties, this guidebook isn't intended for them anyway—it's for people who like to cook and eat adventurously. If you find yourself with a passion for the cooking of a particular country, your local library or bookstore will provide you with enough marvelous ethnic cookbooks to enable you to start specializing.

Throw culinary caution to the winds. Don't try to play

safe and restrict yourself to familiar dishes or familiar in-gredients. If a particular dish turns out to be too exotic and unfamiliar for a guest, don't worry. If a man doesn't like souvlakia (highly improbable), he's still ahead of the game because he's broadened his horizons enough to try it and form an opinion. And nobody has ever been hungry after an Eat-In. The trick is to try everything. The result will be memorable dinners, great fun and if you feel the need to diet, the conviction that you can do it on the other twenty-nine or thirty days of the month.

GREECE

Souvlakia

Sadziki

Greek Country-Style Meat Pie

Stuffed Tomatoes

Beets with Skordalia

Psome

Loukoumades

CAMBRAS "HYMETTUS"
light white wine

CAMBRAS "KOKINELLI"
lightly resinated red wine

Among their other accomplishments, the ancient Greeks are credited with having invented white sauce, brown sauce, Bechamel, the way to filet a fish, and the discovery that oysters are edible. It is the last that is most awesome to me. Certainly it was one of the bravest (or most desperately hungry) men in the history of the world who first bit into an oyster.

The Greeks didn't take cooking lightly. Recipes were compiled hundreds of years B.C. and, like their Chinese counterparts, the Greek philosophers considered cooking of sufficient importance to include their views on the subject in many of their writings. On occasion, however, food and wine did seem to overpower the more cerebral aspects of philosophy. Plato's Dialogue "The Symposium" describes a banquet at the home of a poet where only two guests stayed sufficiently sober to listen to Socrates' words of wisdom.

The elaborate banquets described by the philosophers are as far out of reach for most of the people in Greece today as they were at the time of Plato. The ability to do great things with whatever ingredients are available is not restricted to Greek haute cuisine, however. The Greeks of all classes have a wonderful way with vegetables and a veritable genius with lamb.

Perhaps some apology is needed for the fact that our dessert wasn't cheesecake—another invention of the Greeks and one which they valued so highly that it was used as a ritual offering to the gods and was awarded as a prize in certain contests. (It was, incidentally, frequently baked in the shape of a woman's breast.) Xanthippe, Socrates' shrew of a wife, once in a fit of anger grabbed a cheesecake sent to him by an admirer, threw it on the floor and stomped on it. Notwithstanding this great Greek cheesecake tradition, our own preconceptions prevented us from using it as a finale to the Greek dinner; to us, cheesecake is too irrevocably associated with Lindy's to seem really Greek.

We did, however, stay closer to Greek tradition with the wine. Retsina is a resinated wine. It stems from the days when wine was aged in goatskins and pitch pine was poured on top of the wine to preserve it. The Greeks liked the flavor and continued to use it even after the availability of casks and bottles made the resin unnecessary for preserving purposes. Resinated wine is something of an acquired taste, but the wine which Irwin chose for our dinner is lightly resinated and very good. You can also, if you choose, have ouzo, which is a potent liquor made of grapes and flavored with aniseed. It is usually drunk straight or on ice, but you might try adding a little water the first time around, since most Americans seem to find it a bit strong at first.

We wish you a warm and merry dinner. How can it be otherwise when you're dining on the food of a people whose language has only one word, *xenos,* for both stranger and guest?

SHOPPING SOURCES

If you have difficulty in securing phyllo pastry, kefalotiri cheese or Greek honey locally, here are some sources for you. The phyllo is perishable and should be sent airmail if you live a considerable distance from the source.

AMERICAN TEA, COFFEE & SPICE CO., 1511 Champa Street, Denver, Colorado 80202. Catalogue available. (phyllo)

ANTONE'S, P. O. Box 3352, Houston, Texas 77001. Catalogue available. (Greek honey, phyllo, bamboo skewers)

CHEESE OF ALL NATIONS, 153 Chambers Street, New York, N. Y. 10007. Catalogue available. (kefalotiri cheese)

CHEESE UNLIMITED, 1263 Lexington Avenue, New York, N. Y. 10028. No catalogue available but will fill mail orders. (kefalotiri cheese)

CHEESE VILLAGE, LTD., 3 Greenwich Avenue, New York, N. Y. 10011. No catalogue available but will fill mail orders. (kefalotiri cheese, phyllo)

DELMAN AND CO., 501 Monroe Avenue, Detroit, Michigan 48226. No catalogue available but will fill mail orders for Greek food items.

Greece

SOUVLAKIA

If you will be serving the sadziki as a second appetizer, make only 2 to 3 skewers per person, which is what this recipe will produce. If it will be your only hors d'oeuvre, increase the recipe accordingly.

> 2 *lbs lean, boneless lamb (a cut from the*
>   *leg is very good)*
> 1 *cup olive oil*
> ½ *cup fresh lemon juice*
> 2 *tablespoons oregano*
> 1 *tablespoon thyme*
> ½ *teaspoon salt*
> ½ *teaspoon black pepper*
> 1 *package of small bamboo skewers*

The Day Before

1. Cut the lamb into bite-size pieces—about ¾ inch cubes. Thread 3 or 4 pieces onto each skewer.
2. Mix all the remaining ingredients together. Place the filled skewers in a glass or china dish or an enameled pan and pour the marinade over them. Turn the skewers so that all sides of the lamb pieces are well coated. Cover and let stand at least 12 hours in a cool place or in the refrigerator in hot weather.

Before Serving

1. Heat a charcoal grill, hibachi or broiler until very hot and grill the skewers for 5-7 minutes, turning frequently.

2. While the meat is cooking, heat the marinade. Sprinkle it over the grilled souvlakia before serving.

SADZIKI

We suggest that you serve this dish with a generous garnishing of parsley, not just because it looks pretty, but because the quantity of garlic makes the breath-sweetening parsley advisable if you're going to kiss the children good-night or get within a reasonable distance of anyone other than your equally garlicky fellow diners.

2 large cucumbers
16 oz plain yogurt
salt
6 large garlic cloves
parsley

1. Peel the cucumbers and slice into ¼ inch slices.
2. Place a layer of paper towels in a deep dish and place a single layer of cucumber slices on it. Salt generously. Place another sheet of paper towel on top of the cucumbers, add a layer of cucumbers, salt and continue until all the cucumbers are layered and salted.
3. Cut the peeled garlic cloves into quarters.
4. Put ½ cup of the yogurt into the blender and add the garlic. Flick the switch on and off quickly a few times so that the garlic is finely chopped rather than pulverized.

13

5. Add the blender mixture to the rest of the yogurt and mix well.
6. Remove the cucumbers from the paper towels, cut the slices into quarters and add to the yogurt mixture.
7. Chill and serve.

GREEK COUNTRY-STYLE MEAT PIE

This dish may be made with either beef or lamb. We chose beef, since one of our appetizers was skewered lamb bits. In either case, the meat should be cut into very small pieces or ground coarsely, not ground as fine as you would for hamburger or most other ground meat dishes.

The paper-thin sheets of phyllo pastry can be bought either fresh in Greek bakeries or frozen in many fine food stores. If you buy it fresh, you can freeze it until needed. Be sure it is thoroughly thawed before using.

2 *sticks of sweet butter (½ lb)*
3 *lbs lamb or beef (see note above)*
1 *medium onion, chopped*
2 *cloves garlic, chopped*
2 *tablespoons parsley, chopped*
1 *teaspoon fresh mint, chopped*
1 *cup water*
1 *tablespoon tomato paste*
½ *lb kefalotiri cheese, grated*
2 *eggs, lightly beaten*
  salt and pepper
2 *hard-boiled eggs, thinly sliced*
¾ *lb phyllo pastry*

1. Melt about ⅓ of the butter. Add the onion and meat and cook until lightly browned.
2. Mix the tomato paste with the cup of water and add the mixture to the meat and onions together with the garlic, parsley, mint and salt and pepper to taste. Mix well and simmer for 30 minutes.
3. Remove from the heat and add the cheese and the beaten eggs, mixing well.
4. Melt the remaining butter and set aside for brushing the pastry.
5. Butter a baking pan about 2 inches smaller than the phyllo sheets. Place a phyllo sheet on the bottom of the pan, brush it with melted butter, add another sheet, brush its top with butter and repeat until you have placed 9 sheets on the bottom of the pan. Do not trim the sheets; let the excess go up the sides of the pan.
6. Pour the meat mixture over the phyllo sheets and place the egg slices evenly over the top.
7. Fold the overhanging edges of the phyllo sheets over the top of the filling and brush them with melted butter.
8. Add 9 more phyllo sheets as your top crust, again buttering the top of each sheet before you add the next one.
9. Score the top lightly with a sharp knife to indicate servings. Pour any remaining melted butter over the top.
10. Bake at 300° for 1 hour and let the dish stand for 30 minutes before you cut and serve it.

Greece

STUFFED TOMATOES

(These may be served either hot or cold.)

10 *large ripe tomatoes*
1 *and ¾ cups cooked rice*
¼ *cup onion, finely minced*
3 *cloves garlic, finely minced*
¼ *cup currants, fresh or dried*
 salt and pepper
 olive oil

1. Cut the tops off the tomatoes. With a grapefruit cutter and/or a spoon, scoop out the pulp and put it aside. Salt and pepper the tomato shells and turn them upside down to drain for 10 minutes.
2. Chop the tomato pulp and mix it with the rice, onion, garlic and currants. Add salt and pepper to taste.
3. Fill the tomatoes with the rice mixture. Brush olive oil on the bottom of a casserole and dribble a little more oil over the tops of the tomatoes.
4. Bake, covered, in a 350° oven for 15 minutes.

BEETS WITH SKORDALIA

3 *bunches fresh beets (including greens)*
1 *large onion, chopped*
2 *tablespoons salt*
⅓ *cup olive oil*
1 *tablespoon oregano*
 juice of ½ lemon
 salt and pepper

16

For the Skordalia Sauce

> 10 cloves garlic
> 1 and ½ cups olive oil
>   juice of 2 large lemons
> ¾ cup ground blanched almonds or walnuts
> 1 and ½ teaspoons salt
> 2 egg yolks
> ¾ cup mashed potatoes

To Prepare the Beets

1. Wash the beets, stems and greens thoroughly. Chop the stems and greens, leaving ½ inch stem on the beets.
2. Put the beets, chopped stems and greens, onion and salt in a pot with boiling water to cover. Boil gently until beets are cooked but not soft—about 30 minutes for medium beets or large ones cut in quarters, or 20 minutes for small beets.
3. When the beets are cool, peel and slice them in ⅛ inch slices.
4. Mix the olive oil, oregano, lemon juice and salt and pepper together. Coat the beets with the dressing and refrigerate until 30 minutes before serving time.

To Prepare the Skordalia

1. Grind the nuts in the blender if they aren't preground.
2. Add the egg yolks, half of the oil, the potatoes, garlic, lemon juice and salt. Cover and blend for 15 seconds.
3. With blender still running, remove the cover and slowly add the remaining oil. The sauce should be a little thicker

17

than mayonnaise. If it is too thick, it can be thinned with a little more oil.

4. Chill the sauce. At serving time, put a scoop of skordalia on top of each serving of beets.

PSOME
(City Bread)

> 2 packages dry active yeast
> 1 cup lukewarm water
> 3 tablespoons sugar
> 1 tablespoon salt
> ¼ cup melted butter
> 1 egg, beaten
> 1 cup milk
> 6 cups sifted flour
> 2 tablespoons cream
> 2 tablespoons sesame seeds

1. Sprinkle the yeast and 2 teaspoons of the sugar in the lukewarm water. Cover and let stand for 7-8 minutes until the mixture is bubbly.
2. Stir the remaining sugar, salt, butter and egg together.
3. Scald the milk. When it is lukewarm, add it and the yeast mixture to the egg mixture. Add the flour and mix well.
4. Turn the dough out on a floured board and knead for 10 minutes.
5. Butter the inside of a large bowl and turn the dough ball in the bowl, rotating it so that all sides are lightly

oiled. Cover with a tea towel and let stand in a warm place until double in bulk—about 2 hours.

6. Punch the dough down with your fist. Turn the dough out on a floured board again and knead for 2-3 minutes.
7. Divide the dough into 2 pieces and place each piece in a well-greased 9-inch cake pan or put both loaves on a greased cookie sheet.
8. Brush the tops with the cream and sprinkle with sesame seeds.
9. Cover with a tea towel and let stand in a warm place until the dough doubles again—about 1 hour.
10. Bake bread in a 350° oven for 40 minutes.

LOUKOUMADES

This popular Greek dessert is midway between a cruller and a cream puff. If they are to be made in advance, they can be served either at room temperature or reheated slightly in the oven. In either case, the syrup should be reheated and served warm to be ladled over the puffs.

1 package dry active yeast
3 cups warm water
1 cup warm milk
2 eggs, beaten
1 tablespoon salt
5 and ½ cups flour
2 quarts oil for frying
cinnamon (optional)

1. Sprinkle yeast in 1 cup of the warm water and let it stand covered, in a warm place for 7-8 minutes until it bubbles.

Greece

2. Combine the other 2 cups of water and the milk in a large bowl. Add the yeast mixture, eggs and salt. Stir.
3. Add the flour, mixing well. The batter will be about the consistency of a very thick pancake batter.
4. Cover the bowl with a tea towel and let it stand in a warm, draft-free place for 3 to 4 hours.
5. Heat the oil to 360°. Stir the batter. When the oil is hot, use a large serving spoon to drop the batter into the oil. Make a few puffs at a time so you can turn them occasionally to be sure they brown on all sides. This will take 3-4 minutes.
6. Remove when done and drain on paper towels. Sprinkle with cinnamon if desired while the puffs are still warm.

Syrup

1 lb honey (Greek, if possible)
2 cups sugar
1 cup water
4 thin slices lemon

1. Place all ingredients in a saucepan, bring to a boil and let simmer for 5 minutes.
2. The syrup may be poured over all the puffs before serving or passed in a separate pitcher so that each guest can add his own.

DENMARK

MENU

Aquavit

Danish Marys

Herring Salad

Duck with Lingonberry Sauce

Caramelized Potatoes

Cucumber Salad

Knob Celery Salad

Rye Bread

Buttermilk Bread

Danish Butter

Almond Macaroons

CARLSBERG BEER
dark and light

If there were any justice in the world, the Danes would be FAT FAT FAT. They're not, as a rule, and I wish someone would endow a foundation to discover their national secret of staying reasonably slender when surrounded by the glories of Danish pastry, cookies, cakes smothered in whipped cream, potatoes at every meal (sometimes two kinds at a single meal), creamed soups, yards of irresistible open-faced sandwiches and rich sauces, without which a dish is considered undressed. The Danes do drink their coffee black, but I don't think the answer lies there.

While the Danes don't tend to be fat they do have the amiability that novelists (but not psychiatrists) attribute to the rotund. One of the Antons' most precious memories of Copenhagen is the sight of a group of staid businessmen using one hand to carry attache cases and the other to pelt each other with snowballs. Perhaps because of the cold climate and the unavailability of other entertainment for a large part of the year, the Danes have raised to a delicious high the arts of eating and entertaining. When you have been to a party in Denmark, people don't ask you if you had a good time; they ask you what you had to eat and the answer is usually worth hearing.

A Danish hostess starts her entertaining with a beautifully decorated table. Danish women pride themselves on their ability to arrange flowers, and the table is set with flowers, often little figurines, lighted candles and even elaborately folded napkins. Napkin folding is still taught as part of home economics courses and many cookbooks include a section of instructions on the art of folding. Thus the napkin becomes part of the table decoration rather than

22

a utilitarian part of the service. The quest for visual beauty extends to the food as well as to the table. Meats are carved in the kitchen and every platter which comes into the dining room is carefully arranged and decorated with touches of color provided by radish roses, artfully twisted cucumber slices or some other appropriate garnish.

Someday we'd like to do a Danish luncheon of the traditional smorrebrod—open-faced sandwiches served on thin buttered bread topped with an infinity of ingredients—well, almost an infinity; Oskar Davidsen's famous restaurant in Copenhagen boasts 178 different sandwiches. The smorrebrod is so traditional for lunch that housewives pack the open sandwiches for their children and husbands to take to school or to their offices in special plastic or metal containers designed to keep the tops from getting smeared. For the moment we've resisted the smorrebrod temptation and offer you a Danish dinner instead.

We've added one pragmatic touch to the main course for which you will forgive us unless you happen to have a master carver going to waste in your house. Roast duck, stuffed or sauced with fruit, is very popular in Denmark but it is usually the whole duck which is roasted. Because ducks are difficult to carve and because this method allows you to get rid of most of the fat, we prefer to roast duck cut in parts. It's nice if it's boned, but if your butcher can't or won't bone it for you, simply have him cut it in serving pieces and proceed from there, bones and all.

I'm not sure how or why we included two breads and two salads in this meal. They were all so good we couldn't choose between them. If you have less time or more strength of character, you can eliminate the knob celery salad and one of the breads.

We don't suggest that you try your hand at Danish pastry for the dessert. The many-layered dough is sufficiently difficult for an amateur that even most Danish women, while they are avid bakers of cakes and cookies, tend to buy their pastries at the bake shops.

In the words of the Danish host proposing the first skoal, "Velkommen til bords"—welcome to the table!

AQUAVIT

Aquavit and beer are the Danish national beverages and are frequently drunk together by drinking the aquavit straight and following it with a chaser of beer. You may try it this way if you think a boilermaker by any other name is less lethal. We suggest you stick to straight chilled aquavit and Danish Marys as your predinner drink and leave the beer as an accompaniment to the main course.

Aquavit should be served well chilled and, if you want to do it elegantly, the bottle can be served in a frozen base of ice. Pour about an inch of water into the bottom of a plastic container or a can (an 8-inch high can about 3 inches wider than the bottle is fine). When the ice is frozen, place the bottle in the center, fill the container with cold water and put in the deep freeze for a few hours until the base is frozen. The bottle and ice can be unmolded easily by placing the container briefly in hot water. If you don't have a freezer tall enough to hold a large bottle of aquavit, buy the pint bottles and freeze two of them in slightly smaller containers.

DANISH MARY

For each drink, mix 1 part chilled aquavit and 2 parts chilled tomato or vegetable juice. Please resist the temptation to doctor the drink with spices as you would a Bloody Mary; you'll lose the subtle herbal taste of the aquavit if you do.

HERRING SALAD

You can use salt herring, Bismarck or pickled herring, depending on what your local fish shop, appetizer store or delicatessen can supply. Obviously, you won't want to start with a herring in sauce since you're going to make your own sauce for this dish.

This can be served attractively by placing the herring salad in a mound on a serving platter and garnishing with chopped dill or parsley and 3 hard-boiled eggs which have been separated and chopped so that you can alternate a little pile of chopped egg whites with chopped egg yolks and the green parsley or dill.

Denmark

> 2 *whole herrings*
> *milk*
> *water*
> 1 *and ½ cups boiled potato,* **diced**
> 1 *and ½ cups canned beets,* **diced**
> ¾ *cup apple, chopped*
> ⅓ *cup onion, finely chopped*
> 1 *dill pickle, diced*
> ¼ *cup fresh dill, finely minced*
> 2 *tablespoons white vinegar*
> 2 *hard-boiled eggs, chopped*
> *salt and pepper*

1. Soak the herrings overnight in a mixture of half milk and half water covering the fish.
2. Drain the herrings, and dry with paper towels. Remove the heads, tails and bones and cut the fish in small pieces.
3. Combine the herrings with all the other ingredients, reserving the beet juice for the sauce.

Dressing for Herring Salad

> 1 *cup heavy sweet cream, whipped*
> 3 *tablespoons white vinegar*
> 1 *tablespoon prepared mustard*
> ½ *teaspoon salt*
> 1 *teaspoon sugar*

1. Combine all the dressing ingredients and then mix gently together with the herring mixture.
2. Refrigerate for at least 2 hours before serving.

26

Sauce for Herring

> ½ pint sour cream
> 3 tablespoons reserved beet juice
> 1 teaspoon lemon juice

Stir the beet juice and lemon juice into the sour cream and pass the sauce separately.

DUCK WITH LINGONBERRY SAUCE

> 3 large ducklings (boned if possible) cut in serving pieces
> salt and pepper
> ½ box dried apricots
> ½ box dried pitted prunes
> ¼ cup sugar
> ½ cup water
> 1 cup port (or Cherry Heering or Dubonnet)
> 8-oz jar of lingonberry jam
> juice of ½ lemon

1. The day before you plan to serve the duck, combine the sugar, water and port in a saucepan; stir and bring to a boil. Add the apricots and prunes, cover the pan and let the fruit stand overnight at room temperature.

Denmark

2. Preheat the oven to 350°. While it is heating, salt and pepper both sides of the duck pieces well.
3. Remove the fruit from the marinade. Set the marinade aside and save a few pieces of fruit for garnish. With toothpicks, skewer a few prunes and apricots to the meat side of the duck pieces.
4. Place the duck, skin side up and fruit side down, on a rack in a roasting pan.
5. Bake for 1 hour.
6. Remove pan and drain off fat.
7. Replace the duck in the pan without the rack and continue baking for another 30 minutes.
8. Combine the lingonberry jam, the lemon juice and the reserved marinade in a saucepan. Bring to a boil and keep warm until the duck is ready.
9. Garnish the platter with the reserved fruit and pass the sauce.

CARAMELIZED POTATOES

> 10 medium potatoes or 40 small new potatoes
> ¾ cup sugar
> ¼ lb sweet butter

1. Wash the potatoes and drop them in boiling water, unpeeled. Cook until tender (15 to 25 minutes, depending on size).
2. Remove from water, cool and peel.
3. Cook the sugar in a large skillet over very low heat for

28

about 4-5 minutes, stirring constantly, until sugar turns light brown.

4. Add the butter and continue to cook and stir until the butter is melted.

5. Add the potatoes and cook, turning them frequently, until the potatoes are golden brown and hot.

DANISH CUCUMBER SALAD

If you can find those long thin-skinned cucumbers now being grown in West Virginia, use those and don't peel them. If you have thick-skinned cucumbers, you may prefer to peel them.

6 cucumbers
3 and ½ tablespoons salt

For the Marinade

1 and ½ cups white vinegar
1 tablespoon salt
2 tablespoons sugar
½ teaspoon white pepper
¼ cup fresh dill, chopped

1. Wash and dry or peel the cucumbers. Run the tines of a fork down each side of the length of the cucumber.

29

Denmark

2. Slice the cucumbers as paper-thin as you can and place them on a flat plate (or plates) in a single layer. Sprinkle with salt. Put a plate on top and weight it down with a can or two. Keep at room temperature for about 2 hours; then drain all the liquid off and pat the cucumber slices dry with a paper towel.
3. Mix the marinade ingredients together, except for the fresh dill. Pour the marinade over the cucumbers and sprinkle the dill on top.
4. Refrigerate. Just before serving, drain and discard the liquid.

KNOB CELERY SALAD

This dish really needs knob celery and can't be done with regular celery. You can find knob celery at most really good vegetable markets; don't settle for any other kind.

6 medium celery knobs
1 cup heavy sweet cream, whipped
1 cup mayonnaise
2 teaspoons prepared mustard

1. Peel the celery knobs and cut into the thinnest possible slices. Cut each slice into fine julienne strips.
2. Combine the remaining ingredients and fold in the celery strips.
3. Refrigerate and serve chilled.

RYE BREAD

1 package dry yeast
½ cup warm water
½ teaspoon sugar
1 cup scalded milk
2 tablespoons sugar
1 tablespoon salt
4 tablespoons melted butter
3 cups white flour
¼ cup onion, finely minced
2 tablespoons caraway seed
1 and ½ cups rye flour

1. Sprinkle the sugar and yeast on the warm water. Let mixture stand, covered, in a warm place until it foams and expands—about 7-8 minutes.
2. In a large bowl, mix the milk, sugar, salt and 2 tablespoons of the butter.
3. Mix in all the white flour; then add and mix in the onion, caraway and rye flour.
4. Dust your wooden board with more rye flour and knead the bread for 8-10 minutes until it is smooth and elastic.
5. Grease the bottom and sides of a bowl and turn the ball of dough so that all sides are lightly oiled. Cover with a tea towel and let stand in a warm place until the dough doubles in bulk.
6. Knead the dough briefly, shape into a loaf and place in a well-buttered bread pan. Brush the top of the loaf with some of the remaining melted butter.
7. Cover the pan with the towel and let it rise again until it doubles.
8. Bake at 350° for 45 minutes.

31

Denmark

9. Remove the bread from the pan and place on a wire rack to cool. Brush the top of the loaf with the rest of the melted butter.

DANISH BUTTERMILK BREAD

1 package dry yeast
2 tablespoons brown sugar
⅓ cup warm water
¼ cup butter, melted and cooled
4 cups flour
1 tablespoon salt
2 teaspoons cardamon powder
1 and ¼ cups buttermilk
1 tablespoon melted butter

1. Sprinkle the yeast and sugar on the warm water and let stand, covered, in a warm place until it foams and expands—about 7-8 minutes.
2. Meanwhile, put the flour, salt and cardamon in a large bowl and mix them.
3. Heat the buttermilk until it is warm, but not hot.
4. Add the melted butter to the yeast mixture and then add one cup of the warm buttermilk. Stir.
5. Make a well in the center of the flour mixture, pour in the yeast and buttermilk mixture and mix by working the flour from the sides of the well into the liquid. Beat together well, adding a little more of the warm buttermilk, if necessary, to make the dough spongy and elastic. About 2 to 3 minutes of energetic mixing should do.

6. Gather the dough into a ball in the center of the bowl, cover the bowl with a tea towel and let it stand in a warm place until it doubles in bulk.
7. Knead the dough briefly again, shape it into a loaf and put it in a well-buttered bread pan.
8. Brush the top with the melted butter, cover the pan with the towel and let it rise again until it doubles.
9. Bake at 400° for 20 minutes; turn the oven down to 325° and bake for another half-hour.

DANISH BUTTER

The Danes, less calorie and cholesterol conscious than Americans, use a butter much higher in cream content than we do. Just for this one special occasion you might want to forget your normal qualms and try Danish style butter. You don't need a churn; an electric blender will do.

1 pint heavy sweet cream
½ cup ice water

1. Pour the cream into the blender and blend at high speed until the cream is whipped, stopping the blender once or twice to scrape down the sides.
2. Add the ice water and continue to blend at high speed until the butter starts forming.
3. Put the contents of the blender into a strainer and let it drip until no more liquid is coming out.
4. Gather the butter up in your hands and squeeze and

Denmark

knead it until you have gotten as much of the liquid out as possible.
5. Refrigerate until needed.

DANISH BEER

There are lots of people unconnected with the Danish Chamber of Commerce who think that Danish beer is the best of all the European beers. I happen to be one of them and I suspect that some of the German brewers who import Danish hops for their beers are silently also among our number.

Both the Tuborg and the Carlsberg beers are excellent and you can't go wrong with either. We were lucky enough to find some Carlsberg dark beer, which is less common than some of the light beer. You can, incidentally, enjoy your Carlsberg with a foam of virtue, since the Carlsberg breweries are now owned by a foundation which donates its profits to the sciences, arts and humanities and which helps support such widely divergent organizations as the Royal Ballet and the Institute of Biology.

ALMOND MACAROONS

8-oz can almond paste
2 egg whites
1 cup sugar
candied cherry pieces (optional)

1. Put almond paste in a bowl and knead it with your hands for a minute or two until it is soft.
2. Add sugar and unbeaten egg whites alternately in small amounts, mixing with a wooden spoon after each addition. Blend thoroughly until there are no lumps.
3. Cover cookie sheets with unglazed brown paper (a torn-up grocery bag will do). If you have a pastry tube with a large star head, put the pastry through this. If not, place the pastry on the pan with a teaspoon and flatten each cookie with your fingers. If you wet your hands with cold water, the dough won't stick to your fingers.
4. You can put a small piece of candied cherry on top of each cookie before baking.
5. Bake at 325° for 25 minutes. Remove macaroons to a cake rack to cool.

MEXICO

Have you ever wondered what the history of the world might have been if man had been created without the necessity to eat or if all that he needed for nourishment was easily and equally available in all parts of the world? Starting with Eve's desire for the exotic fruit hanging on that tree in the Garden, a large part of man's motivation to travel, to explore and—alas!—to make war has been directly related to the need or the desire for food.

When Columbus set out to find the short-cut to India, he was primarily interested in spices to preserve food rather than in new or plentiful foods. What he and his successors brought back, however, did more to revolutionize European agriculture and cuisine than the spices he didn't find. Can you picture European cooking without the potato, tomato, eggplant or chocolate? All of these and many others, such as vanilla, beans, avocados, cashews and peanuts were of Mexican origin.

Chocolate was so highly valued by the Mexicans that the cacao bean was at one time used as a form of currency and, like most currencies, it invited attempts to counterfeit. How do you counterfeit a cacao bean? By scooping out the edible portion of the bean and filling it with mud, of course, thereby making what one wag described as "the first hot chocolate."

While Columbus brought cacao home from his fourth voyage, it was the Cortez expedition which succeeded in popularizing it in Europe, aided perhaps by one Spanish historian's report that Montezuma had fifty pitchers of chocolate a day prepared for his own use. Chocolate, vanilla and tomatoes, all brought back to Europe from Mexico, were all for a time believed to be aphrodisiacs. (There's a

38

startling thought to ponder when you treat your children to breakfast cocoa some cold winter morning!) That belief may have accounted for some of the popularity of chocolate and vanilla, but the poor tomato took years to catch on after it had been classified among the poisonous plants by an Italian botanist—nobody apparently wants an aphrodisiac **that** badly.

Until fairly recently, Mexican cookbooks were very rare. Domestic help was cheap and readily available and cooking was left in the hands of people who, by and large, could neither read nor write recipes but worked from direct familial experience and oral transmission of recipes. This is no longer true and in recent years there have been many good Mexican cookbooks published in English as well as Spanish.

I must confess that when Elizabeth, as hostess for the next month's Eat-In, chose Mexico, none of us was particularly enthusiastic about it. Perhaps, as Pat later said, we had been exposed to too many "limp enchiladas filled with gook." We not only ate the dinner; we ate our words. It was a wonderful dinner and we hope you enjoy it as much as we did.

SHOPPING SOURCES

The ingredients you may have trouble finding locally are the masa harina (corn flour), chorizo sausage, fresh ginger and a tortilla press if you want one. For fresh ginger, see the mail order houses listed on p. 65.

ANTONE'S, P. O. Box 3352, Houston, Texas 77001. Catalogue available. (tortilla press)

CASA MONEO, 210 West 14th Street, New York, N. Y. 10011. Catalogue available. (all items listed above)

Mexico

TEQUILA

No Mexican dinner would be complete without a chance to drink straight tequila, Mexican style. Here's how:

For each drink you will need:

> 1 oz *chilled tequila*
> ⅛ *of a fresh lime*
> ¼ *teaspoon* coarse *salt*

How to drink it: Put the salt in the palm of your hand, drink the tequila straight, suck the juice from the lime wedge and lick the salt off your palm.

It may sound odd, but don't knock it until you've tried it. When you're tired of licking your hand, you can have your tequila in a somewhat more conventional drink, the Marguerita.

MARGUERITAS

Have on hand two lemon rinds and a soup bowl with half an inch of coarse salt in the bottom.

For each drink you will need:

> 1   *and* ½ *oz tequila*
> ½ *oz brandy*
> 1 *oz* fresh *lime juice*
> *crushed ice*

40

1. Pour the tequila, brandy and lime juice together and shake with the crushed ice.
2. Moisten the rim of each cocktail glass with lemon rind and then dip the rim into the salt before pouring the drink into the glass.

TORTILLAS AND TOSTADAS

This recipe will make enough soft tortillas to serve with the main course and crisp tostadas to serve with the drinks before dinner.

The tostadas are made by frying pieces of the cooked tortillas. The dough can be rolled by hand but a tortilla press which shapes and flattens the dough costs only a few dollars and is a useful kitchen tool for purposes Mexican cooks may not have thought of—such as making Chinese Mandarin pancakes.

3 cups corn flour (masa harina)
1 tablespoon salt
1 and ½ cups water
½ cup bacon fat or lard

1. Preheat a pancake griddle or a heavy frying pan over a medium flame or heat electric skillet (350°) while you prepare the tortillas.
2. Put the corn flour in a bowl with the salt and add the water, 1/3 cup at a time, mixing well after each addition until the dough has the consistency of biscuit dough.

41

Mexico

3. For each tortilla, use about 2 tablespoons of dough. Roll and pat it into a ball in your hands.
4. Press each ball in a tortilla press or roll it with a rolling pin to a circle about 5 or 6 inches in diameter and about 1/16 of an inch thick.
5. Fry the tortillas on the ungreased griddle or pan for about 3 minutes on each side. The tortillas may be made in advance and reheated briefly in the oven before serving.

To make tostadas:

1. Melt the bacon fat or lard in pan until very hot.
2. Tear cooked tortillas in pieces and fry until crispy and brown.
3. Drain, salt and serve immediately.

AVOCADO SOUP

2 *large avocados*
4 *cups chicken broth*
2 *cloves garlic*
¼ *teaspoon tabasco*
1 *cup light sweet cream*

1. Peel and slice avocados and discard seeds.
2. Put all ingredients, except the cream, into a blender and blend for 15 seconds.

3. Remove blender top and pour cream slowly in while blender is running at low speed. (A little more cream can be added if you prefer a slightly thinner soup.)
4. Chill in refrigerator until serving time.

SAUSAGE STUFFED STEAK

4-4½ lb flank steak
2 *cloves garlic*
½ *cup flour*
3 *tablespoons oil*

Sausage Stuffing

8 *whole scallions, chopped*
¾ *cup walnuts, chopped*
½ *cup parsley, chopped*
4 *teaspoons red chili powder*
¾ *cup bread crumbs*
4 *slices fresh ginger, minced*
2 *eggs, beaten*
1 *lb chorizo sausage, chopped*
1 *teaspoon salt*
½ *teaspoon pepper*

Mexico

Steak Sauce

> 1 and ½ cups tomato puree
> ½ cup dry red wine
> ½ cup beef broth
> 1 bay leaf

1. Have the butcher butterfly the flank steak and pound it so that it is not more than ¼ inch thick. (You may find it easier to make 2 smaller steak rolls rather than 1 large one.)
2. Rub the steak well with the cut cloves of garlic.
3. Mix all the stuffing ingredients together and spread the filling evenly on the steak. Roll up the steak, jelly-roll fashion and tie with string.
4. Dredge with flour and brown the meat roll (or rolls) in the oil.
5. Combine all the sauce ingredients in a pan and simmer for 5 minutes.
6. Put the meat in a casserole or baking dish large enough to hold the roll without bending.
7. Pour the sauce over the meat and bake at 350° for 1 and ½ hours.

MEXICAN CAULIFLOWER

> 2 *medium cauliflowers*
> 1 *stick sweet butter (¼ lb)*
> 1 *cup onion, diced*
> 1 *cup green pepper, diced*
> 2 *lb can tomatoes, drained and chopped*
> 2 *tablespoons chili powder*
> 2 *tablespoons cinnamon*
> ½ *teaspoon salt*
> *No. 300 can pitted black olives, sliced (about*
>   *35 olives)*
> ¼ *cup bread crumbs*
> 6 *tablespoons grated Cheddar cheese*
> 2 *tablespoons butter*

1. Divide the cauliflower into fairly small flowerets and boil in salted water for 9 minutes. Drain.
2. Melt the butter in a saucepan and cook the onion and green pepper until soft but not brown.
3. Add the tomatoes, chili powder, cinnamon and salt and cook over medium flame for 3 minutes.
4. Add the sliced olives and mix thoroughly.
5. Place the cauliflower in a buttered 4-quart casserole and pour the sauce over the top.
6. Mix the grated cheese and bread crumbs and sprinkle the mixture over the top of the casserole.
7. Dot with pieces of butter and cook, uncovered, at 375° for 15 minutes.

Mexico

PICKLED PEPPERS

2 *large green peppers*
2 *large red peppers*
1 *cup olive oil*
¼ *cup white vinegar*
2 *cloves of garlic, crushed*
½ *teaspoon salt*

1. Roast the peppers over an open flame or under the broiler just until the skins are charred.
2. Plunge them into cold water, remove the tops and scrape off the charred skins with a small paring knife. Remove the seeds and cut each pepper into long strips.
3. Marinate the peppers in a mixture of the remaining ingredients at room temperature for at least 1 hour.

PINEAPPLE PUDDING

Before you start, select your serving dish. Choose a bowl or casserole which will just comfortably hold half of the split ladyfingers side by side to cover the bottom of the dish. Choosing the bowl before you jam up the cookies saves you the trouble of testing the size of your dish while you've got a handful of jammy ladyfingers.

24 *ladyfingers, split in half*
 1 *cup apricot jam*
 4 *cups fresh chopped pineapple or canned crushed pineapple*
 1 *cup blanched almonds, ground*
 8 *egg yolks*
 1 *cup sherry*
   sugar (1 cup if you're using fresh pine-apple or ½ cup if you're using canned)
 1 *teaspoon cinnamon*
 ½ *pint sour cream*
   almond slivers for garnish

1. Spread the split ladyfingers with jam.
2. Beat the egg yolks lightly and place them in a saucepan together with the pineapple, ground almonds, sugar, cinnamon and half the sherry.
3. Cook over low heat, stirring constantly, until the mixture thickens. Let the mixture cool for 15 minutes.
4. Place half the ladyfingers in the bottom of the serving dish with the jam side up.
5. Sprinkle with ¼ cup sherry and put half the pineapple mixture on top.
6. Add another layer of ladyfingers, sprinkle with the rest of the sherry and spread the remaining pineapple mixture on top.
7. **Refrigerate for at least 3 hours.**
8. Just before serving, spread a thin layer of sour cream over the top and decorate with the almond slivers.

ITALY

MENU

Fish Fillets with Anchovy Sauce

Spaghetti Carbonara

Osso Buco

Mushroom Salad

Italian Bread

Zuppa Inglese

VALPOLICELLA
light red wine

There are some apocryphal stories that have a neatness to them that makes you wish they were true. Such a one is the legend that Marco Polo discovered spaghetti in the Orient and introduced it into Italy. Not true. There is evidence that pasta in various forms was used by the ancient Romans. Pasta making equipment is preserved in the museum at Pompeii and there are references to various forms of pasta in Italian literature well before Marco Polo set out on his voyages. As a matter of fact, it is far more likely that another European dish, not usually credited to the Chinese, was actually discovered by Europeans in China in the thirteenth century and introduced into central Europe by this means—sauerkraut. The Chinese preserved shredded cabbage in sour rice wine and this may well be the origin of that "typically European" dish.

Larousse calls Italian cooking "the mother cuisine," and even the most fervent Francophile would have to admit that French cooking owes much to its southern neighbor. Perhaps the single greatest culinary missionary from Italy to France was Catherine de Medici who came to France to marry the man who became King Henry II and who brought with her a small army of Italian chefs. Queen Catherine, who has been described as "both a precocious gourmet and a glutton," is credited not only with introducing many Italian foods which have become an integral part of French cuisine but also introducing the fork and the custom of ladies dining with gentlemen—the latter an innovation in a country where co-ed dining was unknown to the gentry.

Someday when the Eat-In runs out of countries, we're going to go back and do it all over again, this time concentrating on regional cooking. The cooking of northern Italy

Italy

is quite different from that of southern Italy and the cooking of Florence is still a third delight. The cooking of the south is what most Americans know best about Italian cuisine and is characterized by the rich use of tomatoes, garlic and pasta, with olive oil featured heavily. The north runs less to pasta and more to rice, cooking is done with butter rather than oil, less garlic is used and the cuisine is somewhat more delicate and less highly seasoned than that of the poorer but lusty south. Florence and its surrounding area is the beef and beans paradise.

Someday we'll do them all, but this particular Italian menu is a little of a number of regional cuisines just as Rome, the geographical as well as political center of Italy, appropriately offers the specialties of all regions.

SHOPPING SOURCES

There are no terribly esoteric ingredients used in this dinner and you will probably find everything you need in your usual shopping area. I can't resist, however, introducing you to some wonderful mail order houses for this or other Italian cooking you may want to do.

ANTONE'S, P.O. Box 3352, Houston, Texas 77001. Catalogue free. (Marvelous selection of noodles and pastas including the hard-to-find ones like spinach lasagna; Fontina, Parmesan and many other cheeses.)

CHEESES OF ALL NATIONS, 153 Chambers Street, New York, N. Y. 10007. Catalogue free. (Fontina, Parmesan and hundreds of other cheeses from all parts of the world.)

CHEESE UNLIMITED, 1263 Lexington Avenue, New York, N. Y. 10028. No catalogue but will fill mail orders for over 650 varieties of imported cheese.

CHEESE VILLAGE LTD., 3 Greenwich Avenue, New York, N. Y. 10011. No catalogue available but will fill mail orders for Fontina, Parmesan and an enormous selection of other cheeses.

FISH FILLETS WITH ANCHOVY SAUCE

10 *fillets of sole or flounder*
salt
pepper
lemon juice
4 *tablespoons butter*
¼ *cup vermouth*

The Filling

4 *tablespoons butter*
1 *cup Italian parsley, chopped fine*
1 *tablespoon garlic, chopped fine*
4 *tablespoons scallions, minced, including green tops*
1 *tablespoon ground oregano*
1 *tablespoon basil*

The Sauce

2 *and ½ cups heavy cream*
2 *tablespoons garlic, finely chopped*
1 *tin flat anchovies, chopped*
6 *tablespoons butter*

1. Wash the fillets and pat them dry. Sprinkle with salt, pepper and lemon juice. Let stand at room temperature for 15 or 20 minutes.
2. Melt the butter in a pan, add all the rest of the filling

ingredients and sauté for 5 minutes. Let the filling cool slightly.

3. Place a spoonful of filling on top of each fillet and roll lengthwise, securing each roll with toothpicks.

4. To make the sauce, boil the cream slowly in a heavy saucepan until it is reduced by about half a cup and is slightly thickened.

5. Melt the butter in another pan and add the garlic, the chopped anchovies and the boiled cream. Heat, stirring constantly until just boiling.

6. To cook the fillets, melt 4 tablespoons of butter in a large skillet, add the rolled fish fillets and pour the vermouth over all. Cover and cook at medium heat for 10 to 15 minutes.

7. To serve, remove fillets to a serving platter and pour the cream sauce over the fish.

SPAGHETTI CARBONARA

6 slices bacon, cut in 1 inch pieces
4 tablespoons butter
2 cups onion, chopped
1 cup parsley, minced
1 cup prosciutto, cut in julienne strips
1 and ½ cups Fontina cheese, diced
4 egg yolks
1 cup grated Parmesan
2 tablespoons hot red pepper flakes
2 teaspoons pepper
2 lbs thin spaghetti

Italy

1. Cook the bacon bits until crisp. Drain on paper towel.
2. Discard the bacon fat and heat the butter in the pan and cook onion until light golden color. Remove with a slotted spoon.
3. Beat the egg yolks.
4. Have all other ingredients cut and ready.
5. To serve, cook the spaghetti, drain it and return it to the still warm pot in which it was cooked. Add the other ingredients and toss quickly but thoroughly.
6. Remove to a warm serving dish and serve at once. Additional grated Parmesan should be available for those who want to add more to their portions.

OSSO BUCO

> 8 *veal shanks*
> 1 *cup flour*
> 2 *tablespoons salt*
> 1 *tablespoon pepper*
> ½ *cup olive oil*
> 6 *tablespoons butter*
> 1 *teaspoon sage*
> 1 *tablespoon rosemary*
> 2 and ½ *cups onion, finely chopped*
> 3 *cloves garlic, minced*
> 3 *cups carrots, diced*
> 2 and ½ *cups celery, thinly sliced*
> 4 and ½ *cups domestic Chablis or other dry white wine*
> 4 *cups chicken stock*
> 1 *small can tomato paste*

For Garnish

6 *cloves garlic, minced*
6 *tablespoons parsley, finely chopped*
4 *tablespoons grated lemon peel*

1. Have the butcher cut each shank into 2 or 3 pieces, depending on the size of the shanks.
2. Mix the flour, salt and pepper and roll the meat in the mixture until lightly dusted with flour on all sides.
3. Heat the oil and butter together (at 350° if you are using an electric skillet for this step) and brown the meat on all sides. As the meat browns, remove the browned pieces to the largest heavy pot you own, placing each piece on its side so that the delicious marrow does not get lost in the cooking.
4. When all the meat has been browned and put in the pot, sprinkle the rosemary and sage over it and add the onion, garlic, carrots and celery.
5. Cover the pot and cook gently for 10 minutes.
6. Mix the wine, stock and tomato paste well and add the mixture to the pot.
7. Cover and simmer for two hours.
8. To serve, remove the meat to a platter. Using a slotted spoon, retrieve all the chopped vegetables from the pot and add them to the meat. Sprinkle with the garnish.

   Note: I suggest that you have shrimp forks available so that the marrow lovers can dig the marrow out of the bones. It's sheer ambrosia.

Italy

MUSHROOM SALAD

2 lbs fresh mushrooms, sliced
3 tablespoons fresh lemon juice
*1 cup scallions (including green tops), thinly
    sliced*
1 tablespoon salt
1 and ½ cups olive oil

1. Sprinkle mushrooms with lemon juice and mix gently.
2. Add remaining ingredients and mix gently again.
3. Refrigerate salad until ready to serve.

ITALIAN BREAD

2 packages dry yeast
2 and ½ cups warm water
7 teaspoons sugar
6 cups flour
1 tablespoon salt
2 tablespoons olive oil
*1 egg white, mixed with 2 tablespoons
    water*
½ cup white cornmeal
   *poppy seed, celery seed, sesame seed
    and/or caraway seed*

1. Sprinkle the yeast and 1 teaspoon of sugar over ½ cup
   of the warm water. Cover the mixture and let it stand

in a warm, draft-free place for about 7 minutes, by which time it will have bubbled and increased in volume.

2. Put 5 cups of the flour into a large mixing bowl. Make a well in the center and pour into it the remaining 2 cups of warm water, the rest of the sugar and the yeast mixture. With a spoon, push in enough of the flour to thicken the liquid slightly.

3. Cover the bowl and set it in a draft-free spot until the center liquid is foamy and begins to bubble in the middle. This will take about a half-hour.

4. Add the salt and olive oil and stir the entire mixture in the bowl vigorously.

5. Sprinkle the entire remaining cup of flour on a board and knead the dough vigorously for 7-8 minutes, working in **all** the flour you have spread on the board. (By the end of the kneading process the dough will have some resemblance to a cannon ball but don't let the heaviness worry you.)

6. Brush the mixing bowl lightly with oil and place the ball of dough back in the bowl, turning it to oil the entire surface.

7. Cover the bowl and let the dough stand for about 1 hour or until double in bulk.

8. Turn the dough out on the board, knead it very lightly and divide the dough into 4 equal parts. Shape each part into a tapered loaf.

9. Sprinkle a cookie sheet with the cornmeal, and place the loaves on the sheet as far apart as possible. With a sharp knife make 3 diagonal cuts in the top of each loaf. Cover the entire cookie sheet with a cloth and let the dough rise again for about an hour until it has almost doubled in bulk.

10. Brush the tops of the loaves with the egg white and

water mixture and sprinkle the top of each loaf with one of the seeds suggested.

11. Heat oven to 350° and place on the bottom of the oven a roasting pan into which you have poured about 2 inches of hot water.

12. When the oven is heated, place the cookie sheet on the center rack and bake for 45 minutes.

ZUPPA INGLESE
(Italian Rum Cake)

Marion Brown is far and away the best baker in our group. Dessert fell to her lot for this dinner and she and husband Bob think this may be about the best thing she ever baked—which covers a lot of territory. The sponge cake can be made a day in advance so that the project becomes less formidable and also gives lots of time for the marsala and rum to soak into the cake.

Sponge Cake

8 *eggs*
1 *and ⅓ cups flour*
1 *and ¼ cups sugar*
2 *tablespoons water*
1 *tablespoon grated lemon rind*
2 *teaspoons almond extract*
¼ *teaspoon salt*

1. Separate the whites and yolks of the eggs. Put the yolks, lemon rind and water in a mixing bowl and beat well. Add the almond extract and stir until blended.
2. Sift the flour together with ½ cup of the sugar 3 times.
3. Sift the flour-sugar mixture once again over the egg yolk mixture. When it has all been added, fold the flour lightly into the yolk mixture.
4. In a separate bowl, beat the egg whites until foamy, then add the remaining cup of sugar and the salt and beat until the whites are stiff.
5. Fold the egg white mixture into the flour and egg yolk mixture.
6. Pour the combined mixture into a 10- or 12-inch ungreased round cake pan.
7. Bake at 350° for 45 minutes or until toothpick comes out clean.
8. Turn the pan upside down onto a cake rack and let cool for at least an hour before removing the cake from the pan.

The Filling

8   *egg yolks*
1   *cup marsala*
8   *teaspoons sugar*
1   *cup light rum*

1. Put the egg yolks and sugar in the top of a double boiler. Beat until the mixture is a light lemon color. Add the marsala and beat until it is well blended.
2. Boil water in the bottom of the double boiler and place the egg mixture over it. Cook for 5 minutes, stirring

constantly, being very careful that the mixture doesn't begin to bubble or boil. Remove from heat.

3. When the custard is cool, slice the sponge cake into 3 layers. Put one layer on your serving plate and pour ⅓ of the rum over the layer. Then spread ⅓ of the custard over the layer. Add the second layer on top of the first and repeat the process. Then add the third layer and the remaining rum and custard.

4. Refrigerate the cake.

Note: Ideally this should be done early in the morning of the day that you plan to serve the cake to give the cake time to soak in the wine and rum.

The Topping

> 1   and ½ cups heavy sweet cream
> 2   tablespoons sugar
> ½ cup glazed fruit, finely chopped

1. About 2 hours before the cake is to be served, place the cream and sugar in a mixing bowl and whip until stiff.

2. Spread the whipped cream over the top and sides of the cake.

3. Make a circle of the glazed fruit around the edge of the top of the cake.

Note: A hint on transporting the cake—Marion put a row of toothpicks on the top of the cake before covering it with waxed paper so that the waxed paper didn't touch and spoil the smoothness of the whipped cream topping. The cake was refrigerated and the toothpicks removed just before serving.

HAWAII

M E N U

Scorpion Cocktails

Shrimp Wonton Puffs

Curry Puffs

Barbecued Chicken Wings

Roast Suckling Pig

Hawaiian Yam Pie

Pão Dolce

Watermelon Basket of Fruits in Rum

Until this century, at least, most of the cities where great food was available were port cities. They had easiest access to foods from abroad and, perhaps even more important, a stream of people from other lands who introduced diversity. The Hawaiian Islands represent an excellent example because so many things which make for the glory of Hawaiian cooking came on the ships which brought Chinese, Japanese, Korean, Philippine and Portuguese laborers, English traders and American missionaries. In addition, the Russian fleet introduced new kinds of alcoholic beverages to the Islands. Where but in a cookbook published in Hawaii would you find a recipe for "Shanghai Corned Beef" served with cabbage sauteed in soy sauce and oil?

Of all the varied peoples who came to Hawaii, the American missionaries seem to have had the least impact on the cuisine. Cakes and breakfast foods were the chief American influence until quite recently. The missionaries may not have succeeded in transplanting the New England boiled dinner, but the American tourist has made New York cut sirloin so popular that some of the hotel restaurant menus make you wonder whether the best place for a Polynesian meal isn't Trader Vic's at the Plaza.

Our menu illustrates some of the diverse origins of the Islands' cooking. The Chinese influence is seen in the wonton, the curries brought by the English traders coming from India are reflected in the curry puffs and the bread is Portuguese in origin. The roast pig is pure native Hawaii, though we couldn't quite duplicate the authentic Hawaiian method of cooking it, which involves an underground oven with sticks on the bottom to burn, porous rocks over the sticks, a mat of leaves, then the food, another mat, more leaves and a dirt covering. Incidentally, when Hawaiian cooking is done outdoors, as it traditionally is, it is the men who do the cooking, not the women. As the smoke begins to rise from the charcoal grills presided over by men in thousands of American backyards, one wonders if there isn't some atavistic aspect in outdoor barbecuing that the sociologists are overlooking.

The most indigenous Hawaiian alcoholic beverage we regretfully had to eschew. This is Okolehao, made from the roots of the ti plant which were allowed to ferment in a canoe "gently rocked with the rise and fall of the tides." We lacked the ti plant, the canoe and access to the gentle tides. The Scorpion which we served as our predinner drink is undoubtedly a conglomerate, but a wonderful one.

Just as Hawaiian cooking has been enriched by borrowing, your Eat-In will benefit from judicious swapping of equipment. While the suckling pig can be made in an oven, if one of your members owns or has access to a charcoal grill with a rotisserie attachment, this is the best way to roast the pig. Similarly, if one of you owns an electric deep fryer, it should be borrowed for the shrimp and curry puffs. The Scorpions were prepared and transported in a large picnic jug with a spigot and served from the same jug.

SHOPPING SOURCES

The only ingredients which you are not likely to find in your normal shopping facilities are fresh ginger root, Chinese barbecue sauce, wonton wrappers and possibly the orgeat syrup. While your butcher can undoubtedly get you a suckling pig if you give him a couple of weeks advance notice, the Maryland Gourmet Mart listed below will ship one if you have trouble buying it locally.

Two tips: Fresh ginger root can be stored indefinitely if it is peeled and placed in a small jar with enough sherry to cover it and refrigerated.

Since the wonton wrappers are perishable, if you live a great distance from a mail order source, try to arrange to have them shipped by airmail.

ANTONE'S, P. O. Box 3352, Houston, Texas 77001. Catalogue available. (Orgeat. Also sells Hawaiian coffee and canned guava, mangoes and kumquats)

FOUR SEAS INTERNATIONAL, P. O. Box 22, Williston Park, New York 11596 or 345 Pennsylvania Avenue, Mineola, New York 11501. Catalogue available. (Fresh ginger root)

KAM SHING CO., 2246 S. Wentworth Avenue, Chicago, Illinois 60616. Catalogue available. (Wonton wrappers, fresh ginger, Chinese barbecue sauce)

KWONG ON LUNG IMPORTERS, 680 North Spring Street, Los Angeles, California 90012. Catalogue available. (Wonton wrappers, fresh ginger)

LES ECHALOTTES, Ramsey, New Jersey 07446. Catalogue 25¢. (Orgeat)

MARYLAND GOURMET MART, 414 Amsterdam Avenue, New York, N. Y. 10024. Catalogue available. (Orgeat, Chinese barbecue sauce, suckling pig)

OYAMA'S ORIENTAL FOOD SHOP, 1302 Amsterdam Avenue, New York, N. Y. 10027. Catalogue available. (Chinese barbecue sauce, fresh ginger)

Hawaii

SCORPION

At Trader Vic's where I first (and frequently) encountered
the Scorpion, it is served in a wide, shallow-bowled stemmed
glass with a gardenia floating on its surface. This adds an
intoxicating aroma to a great drink. We thought of floating
a few gardenia petals on ours but unfortunately with the
prevalent use of poisonous pesticides we couldn't find a
florist who could guarantee that his gardenias were fit for
consumption. If you grow your own or can otherwise be
certain that the gardenias won't put your guests out for
good, it's a nice touch. Not really absolutely necessary,
however. Even without the gardenias, this is as pleasant a
way to get 10 people smashed as you are likely to find.
In fact, this recipe did the job for 12 since two of our
honorary members, Richard Brown and Danny Zavin, man-
aged to get home from college for the Hawaiian dinner.
There is no generation gap where great food is concerned.
Our honoraries refer to the Eat-In as "an over-30 orgy"
and they like it!

> 42 oz good light rum
> 4 oz brandy
> 16 oz fresh lemon juice
> 8 oz fresh orange juice
> 8 oz orgeat syrup
> 3 sprigs fresh mint
> 14 oz domestic Chablis

1. Mix all the ingredients.
2. Add half a tray of ice cubes and let the mixture stand
   for 2 hours.
3. Add more ice before serving.

WONTON WRAPPERS

Wonton wrappers can be bought in the refrigerated food department of a Chinese or Japanese grocery. They can be frozen, provided you let them thaw for at least 24 hours before you use them. These wrappers are good and very inexpensive and we advise you to make your puffs with the bought wrappers if you have access to them. If not, here's how to make your own.

4 cups unsifted flour
1 teaspoon salt
2 eggs, lightly beaten
1 cup cold water

1. Put the flour and salt into a deep bowl.
2. Make a well in the center and pour in the cold water and the eggs. Mix the liquid ingredients into the flour gradually and form the dough into a soft ball. If the dough seems crumbly add more water, a few drops at a time until the mixture sticks together.
3. Turn out on a floured board and knead the dough for a few minutes until it is soft and smooth.
4. Cover the dough with a damp tea cloth and let it stand for 20 minutes.
5. Roll dough as thin as possible and cut into 3-inch squares. The wrappers can be lightly floured and stacked until you are ready to use them.

Hawaii

SHRIMP WONTON PUFFS

> *4 oz cream cheese, softened*
> *6 oz fresh, canned or frozen shrimp, minced*
> *1 clove garlic, minced*
> *¼ teaspoon pepper*
> *⅛ teaspoon Worcestershire sauce*
> *⅛ teaspoon tabasco sauce*
> *½ lb ready-made square wonton wrappers (or use the wonton recipe, p. 69)*
> *Peanut oil for deep frying*

1. Combine all ingredients, except the wonton wrappers and the peanut oil, in a large bowl and beat well until the mixture is soft and fluffy.
2. Place ½ teaspoon of the shrimp mixture in the center of each wonton wrapper. Fold in half over the mixture, making a triangle.
3. Using a toothpick, dab a small amount of the mixture on the surfaces that will be joined together as illustrated, then fold the bottom corners to the center and pinch. The cheese mixture will act as an adhesive to hold the puff together during frying.
4. If the wonton are not going to be fried immediately, cover the uncooked puffs with plastic wrap and refrigerate until ready to cook.
5. Heat at least 2 inches of oil to 375° and fry the wonton, 7 or 8 at a time, turning them, for about 2 minutes or until they are nicely browned.
6. Finished wonton can be kept warm in a low oven (250°).

CURRY PUFFS

  2 tablespoons butter
½ lb very lean ground beef
  1 inch piece fresh ginger root, minced
  2 cloves garlic, minced
  2 tablespoons onion, minced
½ teaspoon ground turmeric
½ teaspoon ground cumin
½ teaspoon ground coriander
½ teaspoon curry powder
½ teaspoon salt
  2 tablespoons lime juice
  2 tablespoons shredded coconut
½ lb ready-made wonton wrappers (or use
    the wonton recipe on p. 69)
  1 egg white, beaten
    Peanut oil for deep frying

1. Melt the butter and add the onions, stirring frequently until the onions are golden but not browned.
2. Add the beef and cook, stirring, until all the beef is lightly browned.
3. Add all other ingredients except the wonton wrappers, egg white and the peanut oil. Stir and remove from heat.
4. Place about ½ teaspoon of the beef mixture in the center of each wonton. Fold the wonton into a triangle and brush a little of the beaten egg white on the surfaces that will be joined together. (See illustration.) Fold the bottom corners of the triangle together and pinch.
5. Fry in deep oil at 375° for 4 to 5 minutes, turning the wonton to brown on all sides.
6. Follow the suggestions given in the shrimp wonton puff

71

Hawaii

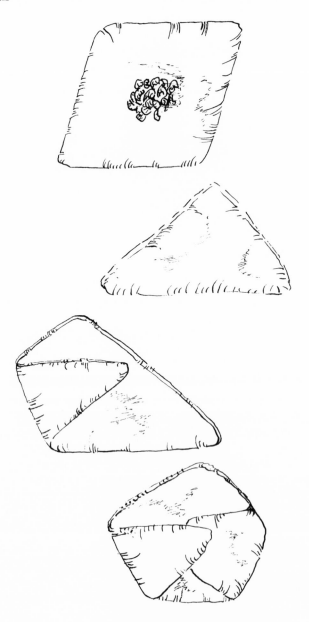

recipe for refrigerating before frying or for keeping the puffs warm.

BARBECUED CHICKEN WINGS

35–40 whole chicken wings
1 bottle Chinese Barbecue Sauce (if not available, substitute a bottle of Heinz Barbecue Sauce With Onions and add 2 tablespoons soy sauce)
3 tablespoons honey

The Day Before

1. Cut off wing tips and separate the joints of each wing with a small sharp knife.
2. Mix the barbecue sauce and honey and marinate the wings in this mixture in the refrigerator overnight.

To Serve

1. Heat oven to 350° and place the chicken wings in a roasting pan. Spoon remaining marinade over the top.
2. Bake for 45 minutes, turning the wings 2 or 3 times during the cooking.

Hawaii

ROAST SUCKLING PIG

> 15 *lb suckling pig*
> ½ *cup lemon juice*
> 1 *tablespoon salt*
> 1 *teaspoon ginger*
> ½ *cup soy sauce*
> ¾ *cup lime juice*
> ¾ *cup olive oil*

1. If you have a paternal butcher (every cook's first require-ment), mix the lemon juice and salt and ask your butcher to rub the inside of the pig with it before trussing it. If you have to truss the pig yourself, remember to tie the hind legs back and the forelegs forward using heavy cord.
2. Mix the soy sauce and the ginger and rub the outside of the pig well with the mixture.
3. Place aluminum foil on the ears to prevent scorching and prop the mouth open with a wooden block if you're planning to serve it with an apple or other fruit in the mouth.
4. A charcoal grill with a rotisserie attachment is ideal. If you're using this method, however, watch carefully and if it looks as if the skin is browning too much, cover the pig with aluminum foil for the last part of the cooking, which will take about 3 hours. Or, the pig can be roasted in a 350° oven, in which case you should allow about 18 minutes per pound or about 4 and ¾ hours for a 15 lb pig. Whichever cooking method you use, baste every half-hour with a mixture of the lime juice and olive oil.
5. When you carve the pig, cut off the small hams first. Then cut down through the spinal column and cleave

off the chops from the ribs and from the loin. Cut the ham into small slices and serve each person some of the ham, a chop and some of the delicious crisp skin.

HAWAIIAN YAM PIE

This pie involves preparing a number of ingredients and then blending them together. For ease, I have broken the ingredients into groups involved in each step.

Group 1: *Preparing the Yams*

> 20 *large yams*
> ½ *lb salted butter*
> 2 *teaspoons nutmeg*
> ½ *teaspoon pepper*

1. Wash the yams and make a slit in the center of each.
2. Bake in a 400° oven for one hour.
3. Cool until they can be handled easily and scoop out the inside.
4. Mash with the other ingredients listed in Group 1.

Group 2: *Preparing the Pineapple*

> *3 tablespoons butter*
> *1 and ½ tablespoons red pepper flakes*
> *1 tablespoon cardamon seeds*
> *1 tablespoon cumin seed*
> *1 clove garlic, chopped*
> *1 fresh pineapple, peeled and cubed*
> *1 teaspoon salt*
> *¼ cup white vinegar*

1. Melt the butter in a medium saucepan and add the pepper flakes, cardamon, cumin and garlic listed in Group 2.
2. Sauté until the butter and spices turn brown.
3. Add the pineapple cubes and mix until they are well coated with the spiced butter. Then add the salt and vinegar.
4. Cover the pan and simmer over low heat for 20 minutes. Set aside.

Group 3: *Preparing the Apricots*

> *1 lb fresh apricots (or ¾ lb dried apricots)*
> *1 cup water*
> *1 cup cider vinegar*
> *¼ cup honey*
> *2 teaspoons paprika*
> *1 tablespoon salt*

1. If using fresh apricots, wash and split them in half, discarding the pits.
2. Place all the ingredients in Group 3 except the apricots in a pan, stir and bring to a boil.
3. Add the apricots, lower heat and simmer for 40 minutes. Set aside.

Group 4: *The Scallions*

5 scallions

Wash the scallions and cut into quarter inch pieces, including the green stalks.

Group 5: *Topping Mixture*

3 tablespoons butter
1 tablespoon coriander seeds
1 tablespoon poppy seeds
1 cup grated coconut

To Put It All Together

1. Mix Group 1 and Group 2 preparations.
2. Grease a fairly shallow baking dish with butter and spread the mixture evenly in the dish.
3. Lay the apricots, cut side down, on top of the mixture.
4. Pour ½ cup of the apricot sauce over the top.
5. Bake, uncovered, in a 300° oven for 1 hour.
6. The dish can now be refrigerated.
7. When you are ready to reheat the dish, melt the 3 tablespoons of butter in Group 5 and add the rest of the ingredients from that group.
8. Cook, stirring for a few minutes until the butter and spices have been absorbed into the coconut and the coconut has turned light brown.
9. Pour the remainder of the apricot sauce over the yam mixture and top with the coconut, sprinkling the remaining tablespoon of scallions on the top at the same time.
10. Cover the pan lightly with aluminum foil and reheat in a 350° oven for 15 minutes.

PAO DOLCE
(Portuguese Sweet Bread)

I have a special fondness for this bread because it's the one that broke my quarter century conviction that yeast wouldn't rise for me. I have finally found the secret (I think). Buy your yeast in the place that sells the most of it so you'll get maximum freshness, close off your kitchen door so you'll get no drafts and don't turn on the air conditioning anywhere within a hundred feet of your kitchen. A little praying helps too.

1 medium potato
2 tablespoons sugar
1 package active dry yeast
¼ cup milk
1 teaspoon salt
¼ cup melted butter, cooled
4 eggs
¾ cup sugar
4 cups flour

1. Boil potato until soft. Reserve ¼ cup of the potato water.
2. Mash the potato and measure ½ cup.
3. When the potato water is lukewarm, sprinkle the yeast and the 2 tablespoons of sugar over it. Cover and let stand in a warm place for 7-8 minutes until the mixture is bubbly.
4. Add the ½ cup of mashed potatoes and mix. Let it stand until it doubles in bulk. (If you do your mixing in a pint measuring cup, this will be easy to keep track of.)
5. Scald the milk; add the salt and cool the milk to lukewarm.
6. Rinse the large bowl of your electric mixer with hot water and dry it well. Break 3 eggs into the bowl. Beat the eggs and then gradually add the sugar, then the butter and then the yeast mixture. When it has been thoroughly blended, add about ⅓ of the flour and all of

the milk. Then add another ⅓ of the flour and mix well.

7. Use some of the remaining ⅓ of the flour to dust a board. Turn the mixture out of the bowl onto the board and blend in the rest of the flour by hand. Knead for about 7 minutes.

8. Wash and dry your mixing bowl and oil it lightly. Form the dough into a ball and roll it gently on the bottom of the mixing bowl so that the entire surface is lightly oiled. Place the ball of dough in the bowl, cover it with a damp towel and let it sit until it doubles in bulk. This takes about 2 hours for me but you might check it after an hour to see if the atmosphere of your kitchen or the efficacy of your prayers produce faster rising.

9. When the dough has doubled, punch it down and divide it in half. Roll each half into a ball if you're going to be baking the bread on a cookie sheet or into two oblong shapes if you'll be using bread pans.

10. Oil your pan lightly unless you're using Teflon. Place the dough in the pan or pans and let it sit again until it has doubled in bulk. This should take about an hour.

11. Beat the last egg and brush the exposed surfaces of the bread with the egg.

12. Bake at 350° for 35 minutes or until nicely browned.

Note: Just for fun, I've left this recipe in the slightly insecure language in which I originally typed it for the other members of the Eat-In. Actually, many bread bakings later, I am now convinced that it wasn't the incantations that did the trick. Somewhere along the line in the more than quarter of a century since I was a bride, the yeast manufacturers have stabilized dry yeast to the point where it is almost impossible not to have your bread rise properly.

Don't take the rising times too seriously. They will vary,

depending on the warmth of the kitchen, the dampness in the atmosphere and similar factors. You can easily tell when the bread has risen enough by poking your finger in it. If the indentation disappears, it hasn't risen enough and should be recovered and let stand longer. If the mark of your finger stays in the dough, it has risen sufficiently and you can proceed to the next step.

WATERMELON BASKET OF FRUITS IN RUM

Don't get neurotic about using the exact combination of fruits suggested. If you have trouble finding one, don't hesitate to substitute an approximately equal quantity of another. It's almost impossible to combine fruit and rum and **not** come up with something delicious.

If you're using fresh fruit and you find that, even with the addition of the watermelon juice, you don't quite have 21 ounces of fruit juice, add enough orange juice to make up the difference.

The basket may be filled with either fresh fruit or canned fruit, depending on what your market has available. In either case, you will need:

1 watermelon, as round as possible
7 oz light rum
grated coconut (optional)

Hawaii

If you are using canned fruits:

> *1 20-oz can of mango*
> *1 18-oz can of guava shells*
> *1 11-oz can of kumquats*
> *1 16-oz can of papaya*
> *1 8-oz can of lichee nuts*

If you are using fresh fruits:

> *2 mangoes, peeled and sectioned*
> *2 papayas, peeled and sectioned*
> *1 avocado, peeled and sectioned*
> *1 guava, peeled and sectioned*
> *1 lb fresh lichee nuts, peeled*
> *1 pineapple, peeled and cubed*
> *2 peaches, peeled and sectioned*
> *1 apple, peeled and sectioned*
> *1 lb seedless green grapes*

1. If you are using canned fruits, drain and reserve the liquids. If using fresh fruit, catch and save all the fruit juice you can when you are sectioning the fruit.
2. To make the watermelon basket, set the melon upright in a snug fitting pot and surround the pot with newspapers to catch juice. Trace the design of the basket on the melon skin with chalk. Starting on the side, cut wedges of melon until the rough basket shape appears, leaving the handle for last. See illustration. Reserve the melon from the cut wedges in a bowl.
3. Scoop out the inside of the watermelon with a melon ball cutter and set the melon balls aside together with

the scooped out melon from the wedges you have cut to make the basket.

4. After the melon is hollowed and the handle is cut, strain the juice remaining in the bottom of the pot and add it to the rest of the fruit liquid. Combine 21 ounces of the fruit juice with the 7 ounces of rum.

5. Chill the scooped out melon, the combined fruits and the rum-juice mixture, all separately, in the refrigerator overnight.

6. Several hours before serving, pour the fruits and the rum-juice mixture into the melon, stir and let it stand at room temperature for ½ hour before returning it to the refrigerator.

7. Grated coconut may be sprinkled over the top of the fruit before serving if desired.

HUNGARY

MENU

Stuffed Cabbage

Hungarian Goulash

Paprika Onions

Cottage Cheese Biscuits

Raisin-Nut Strudel

PUTTONOS, TOKAJIASZU 1964 TOKAY

In 1962 the city of Budapest staged a great festival to commemorate the seventy-fifth birthday of a cake—the famous Dobos torte. This was a most appropriate celebration for a place which has been called "the city of two million pastry lovers." The Turkish invasion of Hungary in the fifteenth century left two lasting culinary marks—the introduction of coffee and the introduction of phyllo pastry, which became the basis for the justly famous Hungarian strudel. The Hungarians are great coffee lovers but it is not clear whether they drink great quantities of coffee because of the availability of superb pastry or whether the quantity of pastry consumed itself creates the demand for coffee. Whichever may be the primary factor, a Hungarian will view any occasion (or none) as justification for coffee and pastry.

Hungarian food tends to be hearty. Bread, noodles and dumplings are important parts of the cuisine. Appetizers play a small role but thick soups are very important. Vegetables dressed only with butter are considered food fit only for invalids or Englishmen; vegetables are normally thickened with flour or with bread crumbs and cream. Pancakes are not generally served for breakfast but are a frequent dinner or supper food, either stuffed with meat or vegetables as a main course or with jam or some other sweet filling for dessert.

Hungarians generally eat a very light breakfast, then have a mid-morning "snack" at about ten o'clock consisting of a small goulash or sandwich. Their major meal is served at lunchtime. Afternoon coffee or tea (accompanied by pastries, of course) keeps body and soul together until light supper is served at eight or nine o'clock in the evening.

If one is entertaining or being entertained (and quite frequently without any such excuse), more pastries and coffee follow later in the evening.

Hungarian goulash probably originated with the herdsmen, who used a single kettle over the campfire in which to cook their meat and vegetables. It is much too good to need a shortage of stove space to justify its continued use. Do make a special effort to use real Hungarian paprika for this dish. It really makes a delicious difference. And if the need for getting the paprika serves to introduce you to two great stores, Paprikas Weiss and H. Roth & Son, either in person or via their mail order catalogues, you will be much enriched. Aside from a fabulous collection of Hungarian foods—pastries, candies, sausages, spices, coffees—the catalogues feature some foods from other countries and the most marvelous selection of kitchen ware imaginable, ranging from noodle makers, cole slaw cutters, fancy cutters for biscuits, cookies and doughnuts, trout pans and on and on and on. I'm waiting impatiently for the Eat-In to get to Portugal so that I can discover what one does with a fascinating little gadget called a "Portuguese Egg-Thread Pourer" that caught my eye in the Paprikas Weiss catalogue. The catalogues will not only supply your own kitchen but will give you years of gift inspirations for every friend who enjoys cooking, eating or both.

SHOPPING SOURCES

AMERICAN TEA, COFFEE AND SPICE COMPANY, 1511 Champa Street, Denver, Colorado, 80202. Catalogue available. (Hungarian paprika)

ANTONE'S, P. O. Box 3352, Houston, Texas, 77001. Catalogue available. (paprika, strudel leaves)

PAPRIKAS WEISS, 1548 Second Avenue, New York, N. Y. 10028. Catalogue 25¢ (paprika, strudel leaves and an inexpensive set of fluted biscuit cutters to which you might treat yourself)

H. ROTH & SON, 1577 First Avenue, New York, N. Y. 10028 or 968 Second Avenue, New York, N. Y. 10022. Catalogue available. (paprika, strudel leaves)

Hungary

STUFFED CABBAGE

You will need either 2 small cabbages or 1 large one to get the 12 large unbroken leaves you need. The rest of the cabbage can, of course, be made into fine cole slaw.

12 large cabbage leaves
6 cups sauerkraut
1 large onion, chopped
3 tablespoons bacon fat
2 lbs lean pork, ground
1 and ½ cups cooked rice
2 eggs, beaten
1 tablespoon salt
1 tablespoon paprika
1 pint sour cream

1. Cook sauerkraut over a gentle flame for 1 hour.
2. Place cabbage leaves in a large pot, cover with water and cook briefly until the leaves are slightly wilted. Drain off water and dry leaves between layers of paper towel.
3. Cook the onion in the bacon fat until golden. Add the ground meat and cook, stirring until it is all browned.
4. Drain the fat off the onion-meat mixture and stir in the rice, eggs, salt and paprika.
5. Divide the stuffing mixture into 12 parts, placing the stuffing on the cabbage leaves and rolling them up as illustrated.
6. Remove half the sauerkraut from the kettle in which it was cooked. Flatten the remaining kraut into a bed, place the cabbage rolls on it and cover them with the sauerkraut which you took out of the pan.

90

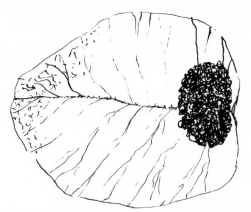

Place meat mixture on lower portion of boiled cabbage leaf.

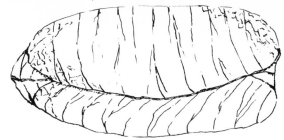

Fold in each side of cabbage leaf toward center to cover meat mixture.

Roll the folded over leaf away from you towards the top of the leaf. Continue to roll until whole leaf is rolled up. You now have a cabbage roll that should stay together. If you are unsure of yourself, insert a toothpick through the top.

7. Cover the pot and simmer gently for 2 hours.
8. Just before serving, spoon some sour cream over the cabbage rolls.

HUNGARIAN GOULASH

2 and ½ lbs beef, cut in large cubes
2 and ½ lbs veal, cut in large cubes
2 and ½ lbs pork, cut in large cubes
18 strips of bacon
2 and ½ cups chopped onion
2 green peppers
8 tomatoes
4 cloves garlic, chopped
7 tablespoons sweet Hungarian paprika
2 teaspoons caraway seed

1. Remove excess fat from meat.
2. Cut the tomatoes in quarters. Cut the peppers in strips, discarding the seeds.
3. Cut bacon into small pieces and cook the bacon bits in a large pot until crisp. Remove the bacon with a slotted spoon.
4. Sauté the onion in the bacon fat until golden brown. Remove with a slotted spoon and sauté the meat in the bacon fat until it is lightly browned. Discard the bacon fat.
5. Combine all ingredients in a large pot and stir. Cover the pot and simmer gently for 1 and ½ to 2 hours. Check from time to time, adding a little water, if neces-

sary, but not too much, since the gravy should be fairly thick.

Note: The goulash can be served with commercial packaged broad egg noodles. Two pounds should be about right.

PAPRIKA ONIONS

3 lbs onions
1 cup bacon fat
¼ cup capers
3 tablespoons sweet paprika
1 teaspoon salt
¾ teaspoon pepper
2 bay leaves
1 cup sour cream

1. Take the sour cream out of the refrigerator and let it warm to room temperature.
2. Peel the onions and cut each one in half from top to bottom. With the cut side of the onion half down, cut each half into ¼ inch slices. Separate the pieces.
3. Melt the bacon fat slowly in a heavy skillet which has a tight fitting cover. When the fat is bubbly, add the onions, salt and pepper and mix. Stick the bay leaves in the center and cover the pot. Cook at low heat until the onions are tender but firm—about 20 minutes.
4. Remove the pan from the heat, remove the bay leaves and drain off the fat. Add the paprika and mix well. Add the sour cream and capers and mix again.

5. Reheat over very low heat before serving. Do not let the mixture boil.

COTTAGE CHEESE BISCUITS

These delicate little biscuits are not difficult to make but the dough needs several periods of refrigeration. Start them early in the day when you know you'll be around for the few minutes it takes every hour or so for the flattening and folding job.

> *2 cups sifted flour*
> *1 teaspoon salt*
> *½ lb cold butter*
> *1 cup cottage cheese*
> *1 egg yolk, beaten with 1 teaspoon water*

1. Sift the flour and salt into a large bowl. Add the butter and cheese and blend with a pastry blender or two knives.
2. Divide the dough into two halves for easier handling and roll each half into a ball.
3. Place each ball between two sheets of waxed paper and, with a rolling pin, roll into a ⅛ inch rectangle. Fold the dough over 4 times as you would a napkin. Wrap in waxed paper and refrigerate for 1 hour.
4. Repeat Step 3 three more times.
5. Roll the dough out ¼ inch thick and cut into rounds with a biscuit cutter or glass.

6. Heat the oven to 400°.
7. Place the biscuits on a cookie sheet, score the tops with a sharp knife and brush with the egg yolk and water mixture.
8. Bake 12 minutes or until tops are nicely browned.
9. Reheat biscuits briefly before serving.

RAISIN-NUT STRUDEL

It takes months of practice to learn to stretch strudel dough to its proper paper-thin state without ending up with a tableful of fragments. Since you won't want to delay your Hungarian dinner that long, we suggest you use the prepared strudel dough that can be bought from one of the mail order houses indicated if you can't get it locally. Once you have the dough, the making of the strudel is unbelievably easy. There are usually four strudel sheets in a package which will enable you to make two strudels—just right for ten people.

> 1 package strudel dough
> 2 cups of ground nuts (unsalted and un-
>   roasted)
> ½ cup golden raisins
> ½ cup sugar
> 3 tablespoons sour cream
>   grated rind of 1 lemon
> ¼ teaspoon cinnamon
> ¼ lb butter
> 2 tablespoons unseasoned bread crumbs

Hungary

1. If the strudel dough has been frozen or refrigerated, allow it to warm to room temperature by leaving it out at least 3 hours or overnight. Do not remove the cellophane or other wrapping before you are ready to use it, since the dough dries out quickly.
2. Melt the butter.
3. Mix the raisins, nuts, sugar, sour cream, cinnamon, lemon rind and 3 tablespoons of the melted butter together. This is your filling.
4. Grease a baking sheet.
5. Place a damp tea towel on a large table. Unfold one sheet of dough and place it on the towel. Brush the dough with melted butter and sprinkle about ¼ of the bread crumbs over the surface. Place a second sheet of dough on top of the first, brush it with butter and sprinkle it with more crumbs.
6. Place half the filling in a 3-inch row along one of the short ends of the dough. Using the edge of the towel to help, roll the dough, jelly-roll style, until it is all rolled up. Still using the towel, roll it directly on to the buttered baking sheet.
7. Repeat the same process with the other 2 sheets of dough and the remaining filling for the second strudel.
8. Brush the strudels with melted butter.
9. Bake at 400° for 25-30 minutes until the strudel is golden brown. Remove to a cool platter immediately.
   Note: If the strudel is not to be eaten on the same day it is baked, it can be reheated briefly in the oven to restore crispness before serving.

ENGLAND

MENU

Christmas Punch

Oyster Stew

Dickens' Christmas Geese

Applesauce

Mashed Potatoes

Granny's Christmas Pudding with Hard Sauce

Roasted Chestnuts

PORT

Our Christmas dinner turned out to be a relatively simple one because our idea was to reproduce the Cratchits' dinner as described in **A Christmas Carol.** This was, it must be remembered, the dinner of a family rich in Christmas spirit and poor in worldly goods. We can only imagine what Christmas dinner must have been like in the home of Charles Dickens whose love for the holiday, joy in living (and enjoyment of an income far removed from that of Bob Cratchit) made a week long festivity of the holiday complete with Charades and other games, amateur theatricals, country dances and, one suspects, food and drink enough to take care of the county. I'm not sure we could have reproduced the bounty of an upper income mid-nineteenth-century Christmas dinner.

For an idea of what such a dinner would have encompassed we can look to two widely disparate sources— Charles Dickens and Agatha Christie. In **A Christmas Carol,** the Spirit of Christmas Present is described as being surrounded by ". . . turkeys, geese, games, poultry, brawn (muscle and flesh of boar), great joints of meat, suckling-pigs, long wreaths of sausages, mince pies, plum puddings, barrels of oysters, red hot chestnuts, cherry-cheeked apples, juicy oranges, luscious pears, immense twelfth-cakes and seething bowls of punch . . . ." Miss Christie's foreword to the Hercule Poirot **The Adventure of the Christmas Pudding** describes the family Christmas dinner at the beginning of the twentieth century. The simple family dinner consisted of oyster soup, turbot, two turkeys (one boiled and one roasted), an "enormous sirloin of beef" topped off by "Plum Pudding, mince-pies, Trifle and every kind of dessert."

Today's Englishmen, reared in the austerity of World

98

War II and its aftermath, must find it hard to believe their forefathers' notion of how much food it took to keep body and soul together. In the sixteenth century, an English Archbishop, perturbed by gluttony among the clergy, issued an edict limiting the clergy's maximum consumption at one meal according to rank. An Archbishop, for example, was restricted to six flesh dishes and four "second dishes." A Bishop might have only five flesh and three second dishes while Archdeacons and Deacons had to make do with four flesh dishes and two second dishes at a single meal.

To today's homemaker it is not only incredible that people could have consumed so much at one meal; it is even more incredible that it could have been prepared even with the ready availability of cheap kitchen help. Catherine Dickens, writing under the pseudonym of Lady Maria Clutterbuck, wrote a cookbook which was published in London in 1852. Here's one of her typical menus for a dinner for 8-10 people:

Vermicelli Soup   Ox-Tail Soup
Turbot and Smelts
Stewed Eels   Soles and Cod's Head
Fricassee Chicken   Oyster Patties   Stewed Kidneys
Roast Sweetbreads
Two boiled fowls   Ham   Pigeon Pie   Saddle of Mutton
Three Woodcocks   Hare   Two Wild Ducks
Mashed Potatoes   Brocoli
Apple Tart   Orange Fritters   Charlotte Russe
Italian Cream
Macaroni   Toasted Cheese

Lest you think that Lady Maria was suggesting ending the meal with pasta, I hasten to assure you that "macaroni" means macaroons. Even so, I know of no ten people who could consume that much food at one sitting and no one who would like to try to turn it out of her kitchen. The Italian Cream alone, for example, had to be hand whipped for nearly an hour.

Our menu for the Cratchits' Christmas dinner is just as described by Dickens with the following exceptions. The Cratchits had no course preceding the goose. We felt that the addition of the oyster stew was justified by the fact that oysters were a very important part of the Christmas dinner of the time. When Samuel Pickwick and his friends set off for Dingley Dell for Christmas, they took with them "a huge codfish" and a "half-dozen barrels of real native oysters." (How's that for a nice portable gift for your weekend hostess?) Moreover, while we think of oysters as a luxury food, they were cheap and plentiful in Dickens' England. As a matter of fact, Sam Weller observed to Mr. Pickwick,

It's a very remarkable circumstance, sir . . . that poverty and oysters always seem to go together and that . . . the poorer a place is, the greater call there seems to be for oysters. Look here, sir! here's a oyster stall to every half-dozen houses. The street's lined with 'em. Blessed if I don't think that ven a man's wery poor, he rushes out of his lodgings, and eats oysters in reg'lar desperation.

While the Cratchits had a gin punch with their dinner, we couldn't resist using the recipe for Dickens' own favorite Christmas punch. The idea for the port and roasted chestnuts for late evening refreshment came from another Dickens source, a short story called "A Christmas Tree."

Just one word about the plum pudding. At the time it is prepared (well ahead of the time it is to be eaten) it is traditional for everyone in the house to take a turn at the stirring. At the same time, favors are put into the pudding,

100

Miss Christie described them as being a ring, a sixpence (now, alas, an obsolete coin) a pig, a thimble and a silver bachelor's button. When the pudding is served the person who gets each favor is believed to have a prediction of his fate. We thought it would be fun to have the favors in our pudding and our tireless London researcher found that Harrods in London sells a little package containing silver favors for the plum pudding. You might want to order them and start a new Christmas tradition in your own family.

Our Christmas dinner was held on New Year's Eve and was a great success. How better can we extend our holiday wishes to you than in Dickens' own words:

Fill your glass again with a merry face and a contented heart. Our life upon it, but your Christmas shall be Merry and your New Year a Happy one.

SHOPPING SOURCES

HARRODS, Knightsbridge, London S.W. 1, England. (Christmas pudding favors. You might also want to order such appropriate delicacies as pickled walnuts and pickled onions from Harrods' famous food shop. Purchases can be charged to your American Express card, thereby eliminating the necessity of translating and transmitting currency.)

PAPRIKAS WEISS, 1546 Second Avenue, New York, N. Y. 10028. Catalogue 25¢. (pudding steamer)

H. ROTH AND SON, 1577 First Avenue, New York, N. Y. 10028 or 968 Second Avenue, New York, N. Y. 10022. Catalogue available. (pudding steamer)

England

CHRISTMAS PUNCH

Our London researcher, Jill Musel, unearthed Charles
Dickens' own favorite recipe for Christmas punch at Dickens
House in London. We've translated it into American terms
and measurements somewhat reluctantly because it loses
some of Dickens' ebullience in the conversion. How prosaic
to suggest a casserole for the mixture when Dickens suggests
a "strong common basin (which may be broken, in case
of accident, without damage to the owner's peace or
pocket) . . . ."

> 3 *lemon rinds*
> 1 *and ⅛ cups sugar*
> 1 *quart rum*
> 2 *cups brandy*
> ¾ *cup lemon juice*
> 2 *quarts water, boiling*

1. Remove as much of the white flesh as possible from
   the lemon rinds.
2. Put the rinds, sugar, rum and brandy into a large sturdy
   casserole and warm slightly.
3. Ignite with either a "wax taper" as the master suggests
   or with one of those wonderful long fireplace matches
   that make it possible for cowards to flambé. Let it burn
   for 3 or 4 minutes and then extinguish the flame by
   putting the lid on the pot.
4. Uncover, add the lemon juice and boiling water. Stir,
   cover and let stand for 5 minutes. You can then taste
   the punch and add a bit more sugar if you like.
5. Recover the pot and let it heat over a very low flame

for 15 minutes. It is now ready to be served. (This last
reheating can be left until just before dinner but if
you're going to let the punch stand for several hours,
remove half of the lemon peel after your tasting.)

OYSTER STEW

3 cups milk
3 cups heavy sweet cream
2 tablespoons butter
1 celery rib, diced
12 salted soda crackers, lightly crushed
3 dozen large oysters
salt and pepper to taste
paprika

1. Preheat oven to 350°.
2. Shuck the oysters; strain and reserve the liquor.
3. In a large saucepan on top of the stove, heat the milk
   and cream to just under the boiling point.
4. Reduce heat to a simmer and add the butter, celery,
   crushed crackers, salt and pepper. Stir well and add
   the oysters and oyster liquor. (If the oysters were pre-
   shucked and you have no oyster liquor to add, substitute
   a cup of bottled clam juice.) Watch the simmering mixture carefully because you don't want it to boil.
5. Just before the stew reaches the boiling point, remove it
   from the stove and pour it into an ovenproof casserole.
6. Bake, uncovered, for 20-25 minutes until the top is
   brown. Stir the mixture and return it to the oven for

another similar period until the top is brown again. Restir and return it to the oven for another 20-25 minute period until the top browns again. (If you'd like the stew a little thicker, you can add another 3 or 4 crushed soda crackers during this last stirring before the final browning.)

7. Dust the surface of the stew lightly with paprika before serving.

DICKENS' CHRISTMAS GEESE

The nature of Mrs. Cratchit's stuffing for her goose is indicated by Dickens' assurance that ". . . the youngest Cratchits were steeped in sage and onions to the eyebrows."

Since we needed two geese (you'd better count on a little unexpected company if this dinner occurs during the Christmas holidays), Marion stuffed one with sage and onions and one with a chestnut stuffing.

2 8 to 10 lb eviscerated geese

Sage and Onion Stuffing

1 cup onions, peeled and quartered for each pound of dressed goose
1 tablespoon crumbled leaf sage
1 teaspoon ground ginger
4 slices soft white bread, crusts removed
salt and pepper to taste

1. Boil onions in lightly salted water until soft but not mushy. Drain.
2. Moisten bread slightly, crumble it and work it into the drained boiled onions.
3. Add seasoning and stuff one goose.

Chestnut Stuffing

> 2½-3 lbs chestnuts depending on weight of goose
> 1 cup soft bread crumbs
> 2 tablespoons butter
> ½ teaspoon thyme
> 1 tablespoon chopped parsley
> salt and pepper to taste

1. Slash chestnuts with knife and cook in boiling water until tender—about 20 minutes. Cool chestnuts and peel them. Chop coarsely.
2. Sauté onion in butter until tender but not brown.
3. Mix all ingredients together and stuff the other goose.

To Cook the Geese

1. Rub salt and pepper on the skin. Pour one cup of water into a shallow roasting pan.
2. Place geese, breast sides up, on a rack in the roasting pan and roast at 325°.
3. Spoon off fat from pan from time to time and baste the geese at the same time. An 8-pound goose will roast in

105

England

4 hours and a 10-pound one will take about 5 hours. When the geese are done, the drumsticks will move up and down freely and the skin will be well browned and crisp.

APPLESAUCE

Poor Mrs. Cratchit didn't have a blender or one of those marvelous gadgets that core and cut apples into wedges with one stroke. We suggest you use both; you have all the disadvantages of our century so you might just as well enjoy the benefits.

> 2 *lbs Macintosh apples, unpeeled and diced*
> 1 *cup water*
> ½ *cup sugar*
> 1 *tablespoon cinnamon*

1. Put all ingredients into the blender and blend for about 30 seconds.
2. Pour into a saucepan and heat the applesauce just until it boils.
3. Cool and refrigerate.

MASHED POTATOES

You obviously don't need a recipe for mashed potatoes. Our one suggestion is that if the vegetable cook can coordinate with the goose cook, it's nice to use rendered goose fat instead of the butter you might normally mix into the potatoes.

GRANNY'S CHRISTMAS PUDDING

Jane Grogan, to whom we are indebted for this recipe, insists that it be made at least three weeks ahead and that the cook follow the old English custom of having everyone in the house take a turn at stirring the pudding. Don't omit the stirring party; for all we know it really contributes to the delicious results.

You can buy a pudding steamer at one of the sources listed at not too great a cost and it may be a worthwhile investment if this easy but great pudding is likely to become a tradition in your house. You can, however, use any sturdy bowl that holds about 2 quarts and a pint. (I used a Dansk bean pot set inside my old baby bottle sterilizer, just to give you one idea of improvisation.)

The pudding is steamed by buttering the inside of the bowl before putting the pudding into it, then placing waxed paper and aluminum foil over the top of the bowl and tying a string around the foil to keep it tight. The bowl is then placed on a trivet or a small upside down cake pan in a large pot. Put boiling water in the pot until it is about two thirds up the side of the bowl and cover the pot. Additional boiling water may have to be added from time to time.

England

3-4 Weeks Before Serving

> 3 *cups dried currants*
> 2 *cups golden raisins*
> 2 *cups black, seedless raisins*
> ¾ *cup mixed fruit peel*
> 1 *and* ⅛ *cup brown sugar*
> ¾ *cup rum*
> 1 *apple*
> ¾ *cup blanched almonds, chopped*
> 1 *cup unseasoned bread crumbs*
> 1 *teaspoon cinnamon*
> ½ *teaspoon mace*
> 3 *large eggs*
> 2 *cups flour*
> ¼ *cup suet, cut in small pieces*
> 1 *teaspoon salt*

1. Peel and grate apple. Cut the fruit peel into small pieces.
2. Put all the fruit in a large bowl, add the sugar and the rum and allow the fruit to soak in the rum overnight.
3. The next day, add all other ingredients, mix well, cover the bowl and place it in a cool place for 3-4 weeks. (The bottom shelf of the refrigerator is safest for Americans who live with central heating.)

To Steam the Pudding

Steam for 6 hours according to the method described in the introductory note. To serve the pudding, run a sharp knife around the inside of the bowl, place a serving plate on top of the bowl and invert.

There are two schools of thought on the sauce to serve with a Christmas pudding—custard sauce or hard sauce. As you can see, we vote for the latter.

Hard Sauce

1 cup heavy sweet cream
3 tablespoons rum
2 cups confectioner's sugar
¼ lb. butter, softened to room temperature

1. Place the cream, rum and 1 cup of the sugar in a blender and blend at high speed for 15 seconds.
2. Add the butter and the remaining cup of sugar and blend at high speed for 30 seconds or until the butter has disappeared.
3. Pour the sauce into a serving bowl, cover and refrigerate for 6 or 7 hours before serving.

INDIA

MENU

Papadam with Apple Sambal

Pakoras

Lamb Soup

Lamb with Condiments

Rice and Vegetable Pilaf

Indian-Style Lentils

Paratha

Naan

Cheese Balls

Hima Gulab Jamun

BALLANTINE "INDIA" PALE ALE

In Pearl Buck's book, **Mandala,** the Maharana says to his American friend, "Our food is execrable unless it is cooked in Indian fashion and all the flavors hidden in chili and pepper." The poor quality of the basic food—meat in particular—may be one explanation of why spices became so important a feature of Indian cooking but it is hardly the only one, or even the most convincing. In a hot climate the preservative qualities of spices are very important and the Indians had available to them easily and cheaply the same spices for which Europeans sent ships on costly and dangerous voyages and which were an expensive luxury when they reached their destination. Under these circumstances it would have been astonishing if English food were characterized by spiciness and Indian food by blandness.

Whatever the reasons, the arts of spice mixing and cooking with spices have been developed to their fullest in Indian cooking. In some places a stone mortar and pestle are a traditional part of a bride's trousseau. The bride's ability to make masalas, combinations of ground spices, are an important part of her role as the mistress of the household. Santha Rama Rau points out that her Indian friends and relatives hire a cook on the basis of a trial dish which not only tests his ability to grind the spices properly but to cook it in a way that brings out the maximum flavor.

Indian cuisine is affected by a variety of religious prohibitions. The Hindus will not eat meat of any kind because of their belief in the transmigration of souls. Some vegetarians refuse even to eat root vegetables because the process of pulling such things as potatoes or carrots out of the ground might cause the accidental death of an earthworm or insect. Pork is shunned by the Muslims. For both

112

religious and economic reasons, vegetables are of primary importance. For nonvegetarians the chief meat is lamb.

If you want to serve your dinner in authentic Indian fashion, you will not serve it in courses. All the food, including dessert, will be placed on the table at one time and each guest will choose what combinations he will eat. No cutlery will be used. If you're eating Southern fashion, each diner will help himself with the fingers of his right hand; if you're eating Northern style, the food will be picked up and conveyed to the mouth on torn off pieces of bread. If you're going to go all the way in following tradition you will serve the husbands and male guests first, then the children, and the women will eat last of all. I think this concept could be sold to American women only with an ironclad guarantee that the men would be cleaning up the kitchen while the women are eating. If you can't drive that kind of bargain at least, you will probably prefer to mix a little American dining custom with your Indian dinner.

You will note that the menu lists lamb soup but that there is no recipe for it. You're not missing a page of the book; the soup is a by-product of the main course.

A word on the subject of Indian desserts: The most frequently encountered desserts tend to be either a variety of rice pudding, which we did not want to use since we had a large rice dish as one of the vegetable courses, or small bite-sized morsels so sweet that they make your bridges ring. While both our desserts were poached in the omnipresent sugar syrup, they are less sweet than most Indian desserts and more acceptable to the American palate.

The Hima Gulab Jamun was made from a package of Hima Gulab Jamun Mix purchased from the Orient Export Trading Co. and is definitely worth ordering when you are buying the rest of the ingredients you will need for the meal. You can follow the directions on the package except that, while the directions specify deep-frying in Dalda, you can use any vegetable oil heated to 300°.

SHOPPING SOURCES

AMERICAN TEA, COFFEE AND SPICE COMPANY, 1511 Champa Street, Denver, Colorado 80202. Catalogue available. (papadam, chick pea flour, rose water, prepared ghee, canned Gulabjimin)

ANTONE'S, P. O. Box 3352, Houston, Texas 77001. Catalogue available. (papadam, rose water, canned ghee)

ANTONE'S IMPORT FOODS, 2606-K South Sheridan Rd., Tulsa, Oklahoma 74129. No catalogue available but carries a good variety of Indian ingredients.

BEZJIAM'S GROCERY, INC., 4725 Santa Monica Blvd., Los Angeles, California 90029. Catalogue available. (papadam, garamasala, rose water, ghee, whole wheat flour)

KALUSTYAN'S, 123 Lexington Avenue, New York, N. Y. 10016. Catalogue available. (all ingredients needed for the menu)

LES ECHALOTTES, Ramsey, New Jersey 07446. Catalogue 25¢. (papadam, rose water)

ORIENT EXPORT TRADING CO., 123 Lexington Avenue, New York, N. Y. 10016. Catalogue available. (Hima gulab jamun mix, papadam)

PAPRIKAS WEISS, 1546 Second Avenue, New York, N. Y. 10028. Catalogue 25¢. (papadam, rose water)

TRINACRIA IMPORTING CO., 415 Third Avenue, New York, N. Y. 10016. Partial catalogue available but store carries many items not listed. (All needed ingredients available here)

For sources of fresh ginger, see P. 67

India

GHEE

Ghee is in effect a super-clarified butter. It has a taste all its own and no lover of Indian food would consider ordinary butter an effective substitute. Its original popularity, however, was probably less attributable to its flavor than to the fact that butter rendered in this fashion will keep without refrigeration for 2 to 3 months.

A full pound of butter is about what will be needed for all the recipes which call for ghee. The breads alone require ghee made from a half pound of butter. You may find it convenient to have one member of the Eat-In make the ghee for all the cooks. If this is inconvenient, you can make it up individually, keeping in mind that a quarter pound stick of sweet butter will produce about 5 or 6 tablespoons of ghee.

1. In your heaviest large saucepan heat the butter over low heat, being sure that it does not brown as it melts. When it is all melted, increase the heat and cook until the butter boils and is covered with white foam.

2. Reduce the heat to very, very low, stir the butter once and then let it cook, uncovered, without further stirring for 45 minutes. At this point the solids will have formed on the bottom of the pan and the liquid on top will be clear.

3. Line your sieve with a linen dish towel or several layers of cheesecloth and pour the clear liquid through the sieve into a large bowl. Strain a second time if any solids slip through.

4. The ghee can now be poured in a jar and either refrigerated or kept at room temperature until needed.

Note: Pat, who is our most frequent and talented Indian

116

cook, refrigerates and uses the leftover solids to season whatever meat or vegetable dishes she may be making in the few days after she makes the ghee. It lends a nutty-buttery taste to food.

PAPADAM WITH APPLE SAMBAL

Papadam is a very thin crisp fried bread which, like most Indian breads, is designed to be used as a scoop for other foods rather than as an individual food. Since the bread-maker for this meal already has two things to prepare, we suggest you buy the papadam packaged and ready for brief frying in oil. While you're ordering, we strongly suggest that you order a couple of packages of Red Chillis Paparh, a spicy version which keeps well and which you may want to have on hand even for non-Indian cocktail parties. The cocktail "dip" is relatively new in American entertaining but, as you can see, the Indians have been using it for centuries—usually, I hasten to add, without any alcoholic accompaniment.

Apple Sambal

> 2 large tart apples
> 1 small onion
> ½ teaspoon ground ginger
> 2 tablespoons ghee
> 1 teaspoon lemon juice
> salt and pepper
> 1 cup yogurt

117

India

1. Peel the apples and dice them into tiny cubes. Mince the onion.
2. Heat the ghee in a small saucepan and add the diced apples, minced onions and ginger.
3. Sauté gently until soft but not mushy. Add the lemon juice and salt and pepper to taste.
4. When cool, mix in yogurt and refrigerate until needed.

PAKORAS

½ cup chick pea flour (besan)
¼ teaspoon baking powder
⅔ cup water
1 medium onion, finely minced
½ cup finely diced raw potato or eggplant
  or zucchini
½ teaspoon paprika
1 teaspoon salt
3 cups vegetable oil

1. Blend the flour, baking powder and water until smooth.
2. Add all the rest of the ingredients except the oil and stir until well mixed.
3. In an electric skillet or deep fryer, heat the oil to 350°. While it is heating, make about 20 small balls with the batter and then flatten each ball slightly.
4. Drop into the oil a few at a time so that the temperature of the oil does not drop. Turn the fritters once during the frying process. They will fry to a nice golden brown in about 7 minutes.

INDIAN LAMB
(With soup thrown in as a bonus)

This lamb is partially made the day before it is to be served, since it needs to marinate for 24 hours before it is cooked. You will note that instructions throughout refer to use of a blender which may strike you as lacking true Indian authenticity. It does. In the absence of a blender, you could in theory use a grater, a mortar and pestle and untold energy. The Indian ladies do, but I for one have no ambition to follow their example.

The Day Before

> Large leg of lamb, 8 to 9 lbs
> 10 cloves of garlic
> 8 cloves
> ¾ cup fresh lemon juice
> 1 and ½ tablespoons salt
> 1 and ½ tablespoons red pepper flakes
> 1 and ½ tablespoons turmeric
> 1 and ½ tablespoons cumin seed
> 6 inch cinnamon stick, broken
> ½ teaspoon cardamon pod seeds
> 1 and ½ tablespoons fresh ginger root, peeled and coarsely chopped

1. Have the butcher remove all the fat and the fell from the lamb. There must be absolutely no fat if you are to be able to use as a soup the liquid in which the lamb is cooked.
2. Peel and sliver the garlic. Make ½ inch gashes in the

119

lamb and insert the garlic slivers. Stick the cloves into the lamb.
3. Put all other ingredients into your blender and blend briefly at high speed. Rub the blender mixture well into the lamb. Place the lamb in a very large pot; cover it and let it marinate for an hour at room temperature.

The Marinade

12 oz blanched peanuts
2 cups yogurt
1 cup seedless raisins
1 cup honey

1. Soak the raisins in half a cup of water to soften them.
2. Grind the peanuts in the blender.
3. Remove to a bowl, add the yogurt and the raisins, discarding the water in which the raisins have been softened.
4. Pour half of this mixture over one side of the lamb and then pour half of the honey over the same side. Turn the lamb over and repeat on the other side.
5. Cover the lamb and let it marinate in a cool place (not the refrigerator) for 24 hours.

The Day of the Dinner

Coconut Milk

Buy either 1 large or 2 small coconuts. This will give you enough coconut meat, not only for the coconut milk in which you will cook the lamb, but for the Banana and Coconut Foogath which you will serve as an accompaniment to the lamb.

3 cups coconut meat, cut in large pieces
3 cups boiling water

1. Remove all brown skin before measuring coconut. Place one cup of coconut meat and 1 cup of boiling water in the blender and blend at high speed for 2 minutes. Remove to a large bowl.
2. Repeat the blending process twice more using 1 cup of coconut and 1 cup of water each time.
3. Let the blended coconut and water rest in the bowl for about 45 minutes.
4. Using a fine sieve, strain the liquid into another bowl, pressing all the liquid out of the coconut grains with the back of a wooden spoon. Discard the grains.
5. Preheat the oven to 350°. While it is heating, pour the coconut milk into a saucepan and heat it to the boiling point.
6. Pour the coconut milk over the lamb.
7. Cover and bake for 2 and ½ hours.
8. Reduce oven heat to 150°, remove the cover and continue roasting for 3 hours longer.
9. The lamb can now be removed to a warm platter. It will remain ready to serve for a full hour.
10. The liquid in which the lamb was cooked can be reheated if necessary before serving as a separate soup course. A dollop of yogurt floated on top of each bowl of soup is a nice final touch.

India

CONDIMENTS

These three condiments are all easy and quick to prepare. They should not, however, be refrigerated so it is best to make them the day they are to be served and let them stand at room temperature. You can, of course, refrigerate any leftovers for later use.

Green Ginger Chutney

½ cup fresh ginger root, peeled and cubed
¼ cup cider vinegar
¼ cup chopped onion
¼ cup white raisins
½ cup brown raisins

Place all ingredients in blender and blend at high speed.

Avocado Chutney

2 ripe avocados
¼ cup lemon juice
½ teaspoon cumin powder
½ teaspoon black pepper
1 teaspoon salt
1 tablespoon grated onion

1. Peel the Avocado and cut into slices.
2. Mix the remaining ingredients and pour the mixture over the avocado slices, turning to cover both sides of the slices.

Banana and Coconut Foogath

> 3 bananas, not quite ripe
> 2 tablespoons vegetable oil
> 1 teaspoon ground coriander
> juice of ½ lemon
> ¼ cup ghee
> 1 and ½ teaspoons red pepper flakes
> 4 tablespoons black mustard seeds (also known as rape)
> 1 cup freshly grated coconut

1. Slice the bananas and mix the slices with the oil, coriander, mustard, and lemon juice. Salt and pepper to taste.
2. Heat the ghee in a saucepan. When it is sizzling, add the coconut. Cook, stirring constantly until the coconut is slightly brown and has absorbed the ghee.
3. Remove the coconut from the heat, cool it slightly and add it to the banana mixture.

India

RICE AND VEGETABLE PILAF

6 tablespoons ghee
1 cup onions, diced
2 cups white rice
4 cups fresh or frozen vegetables (string beans, peas, sliced carrots, green pepper slaces or what-have-you)
5 cups water
1 and ½ tablespoons salt
1 teaspoon garam masala
1 teaspoon dried coriander

1. Heat 4 tablespoons of the ghee in a large heavy saucepan or Dutch oven. When it is barely sizzling, add the diced onion and sauté gently until the onion is golden but not brown.
2. Add the rice and stir well, then add all remaining ingredients except for the two remaining tablespoons of ghee and the coriander.
3. Cover the pan tightly. Cook for 20 minutes. All the liquid should be absorbed.
4. After the pilaf has been placed on a serving platter, sprinkle the remaining ghee and the coriander over the top.

INDIAN STYLE LENTILS

We have our doubts as to whether canned onion soup plays much of a part in Indian cuisine but we may be wrong. After all, it is startling to walk into the elegance of Fortnum and Mason in London and see that the glamorous "Foreign Foods" section features such exotica as Hellman's Mayonnaise and Campbell's soups. Whether canned onion soup is popular in New Delhi or not, for this recipe, canned soup is thoroughly satisfactory.

> 1 package lentils (1 lb)
> 2 cans condensed onion soup (10½-oz size)
> 3 cups water
> ½ cup olive oil
> 2 teaspoons salt
> ½ teaspoon pepper
> 2 tablespoons parsley, finely chopped

1. Wash lentils thoroughly and drain.
2. Combine all ingredients in a large saucepan and simmer, uncovered, for 1 hour or until lentils are tender and liquid is almost absorbed.
3. Can be served either hot or cold.

PARATHA
(Fried whole wheat bread)

> 2 cups whole wheat flour
> 1 and ½ cups ghee
> ½ cup cold water

1. Combine the flour and about 2 tablespoons of ghee in a bowl. Rub the flour and ghee together with your fingers until the mixture is grainy.
2. Add the water and mix.
3. Use additional water if necessary to form the dough into a ball. Knead the dough on a lightly floured board until it is elastic and smooth—about 7 minutes of steady kneading.
4. Place the ball of dough in a bowl, cover with a cloth and let it sit for half an hour. Meanwhile, melt the rest of the ghee.
5. Divide the dough into 8 equal parts. To shape the individual breads, place each portion of dough on a lightly floured board and, with a rolling pin, roll it out to a 7-inch circle.
6. Brush the top with about a teaspoon of ghee and then fold the round in half. Brush the top again with ghee and fold it in half once more. At this point you should have a triangle with a curved edge. Roll it gently with the rolling pin to flatten it slightly.
7. A Teflon lined skillet or electric frying pan is best for frying the breads, but you can use a griddle or a cast-iron skillet, greasing it as lightly as possible with ghee. Heat the pan or griddle (350° if you're using an electric pan). Put as many of the breads as your pan will hold into the pan and cook until the top is speckled with brown, moving the breads during the cooking so they don't stick.
8. Turn the breads with a spatula and brush the cooked side with more of the ghee. Cook for 2 minutes more, turn the breads once again and spread the tops with more ghee and cook for 1 minute more.
9. If made ahead of time, the paratha can be warmed in

an ungreased skillet or in the oven very briefly before serving.

NAAN
(Indian Bread)

> 4 cups flour
> 1 tablespoon sugar
> 1 tablespoon baking powder
> ¼ teaspoon baking soda
> ½ teaspoon salt
> 2 eggs
> 1 cup milk
> 4 to 6 teaspoons ghee

1. Combine the flour, sugar, baking powder, baking soda and salt in a large mixing bowl and stir until well blended.
2. Make a shallow well in the center of the mixture and drop the eggs in. Stir until blended and add milk a little at a time, stirring.
3. Gather the dough into a ball and put it on a large china platter, cookie sheet or other smooth surface. Knead the dough for ten minutes until it is smooth. You can sprinkle a little flour on the dough from time to time during the kneading to keep the dough from sticking to your hands.
4. Take about a teaspoon of the ghee and moisten your palms with it. Gather the dough into a ball and place it in a bowl covered with a cloth, away from drafts for about 3 hours.

127

5. Put two ungreased baking sheets into the oven and pre-heat the oven to 450°. While it is heating, divide the dough into 6 equal portions, using more ghee to moisten your hands from time to time while you're handling the dough. Flatten each of the six portions of dough into a teardrop shape. Flatten the inner part of each shape slightly so that your bread will be a little higher at the sides than in the middle.
6. Put the loaves on the baking sheets and bake for 6 minutes. Then slide each sheet under the broiler for a minute to lightly brown the tops of the loaves.
7. The breads can be served warm or at room temperature. We prefer them warmed in the oven before serving.

INDIAN CHEESE BALLS

1 lb farmer cheese
2 tablespoons quick or instant farina
4 cups water
2 cups sugar
2 pinches cream of tartar
fresh mint leaves
2 teaspoons rose water

1. Let cheese soften to room temperature.
2. Transfer it to a large flat plate, teflon cookie sheet, marble slab or other smooth surface and knead it for 2 minutes with the heel of your hand as if kneading bread.
3. Add the farina.
4. Combine the water, sugar, cream of tartar and 4 mint

sprigs in a pan. Bring to a boil and let it boil until it thickens slightly—about 10 minutes.

5. While the syrup is boiling, knead the cheese-farina mixture until the cheese is firm and doesn't crumble.

6. Divide into 12 balls, each of which will be a little smaller than a golf ball.

7. Reduce the heat of the syrup and drop the balls into the syrup. Cook for 45 minutes in simmering syrup, basting the balls from time to time with the syrup.

8. Remove from heat and let cool for 10 minutes.

9. Remove the cheese balls. Strain the syrup and add the rose water to the clear syrup. Store the balls in the syrup in the refrigerator.

10. To serve, put each ball into a dessert dish or a fluted paper muffin cup, pour a little syrup over it and decorate with mint leaves.

FRANCE

MENU

Country Pâté

Assorted Hors D'Oeuvres

Bouillabaisse

Ratatouille

French Bread

Demi-Mousse with Meringues

POUILLY-FUISSE

I don't usually think of myself as a timid soul. I'm only frightened by the things that any sensible person would be intimidated by—mice, hospital nurses, people who speak five languages fluently (and who, I am sure, are saying deprecatory things about my ignorance in at least four of them), dentists. . . . Come to think of it, I'm intimidated by quite a lot of things. But one of them is people who write about French cooking and who have the knack of making the hapless reader feel that only a savage would use powdered chicken bouillion instead of cooking a whole hen to get the half cup of bouillion called for by the recipe.

I'm beginning to believe, however, that some of the intimidation is the result of a deliberate effort on the part of the experts on French cuisine. As I cringed through a recent popular book on the subject, I suddenly began to wonder why the author devoted quite so much time to stressing that the French wouldn't **dream** of drinking coffee throughout lunch or dinner. I don't know many Americans who do either but nobody makes a virtue of it in praising our gustatory sense.

On the other hand, to be just, some of the excellence of French cooking is undoubtedly attributable to the fact that the French **care** enough to be terribly fussy about the freshness and the quality of the ingredients that go into the pot. Les Halles, the famous Paris food market which had its origins in the twelfth century, has changed its location from time to time but has never changed the basic rule that any food unsold on the day it comes to market cannot be held over for sale the next day. French women are still willing to let shopping take a large chunk out of each day by not shopping in advance and by going from specialized

132

store to store to get the best available ingredients. What can you say about people who not only won't eat packaged bread but who think that yesterday's fresh baked bread is only fit to be used in cooking? (You will notice, incidentally, on the subject of bread that we rushed in where angels fear to tread. Many French cookbooks published in the United States give no recipe for French bread on the grounds that it can't be made without French flour and/or a French baker's oven. Elizabeth made it and we liked it.)

It may be that some of the glory of French home cooking will pass as the country becomes more urbanized, the long lunch is sacrificed in favor of the long weekend, and more women join the labor market. I have the comforting feeling, however, that the standards will stay high. If you want proof, the next time you're in France, sneak away from the museums long enough to wander through one of the supermarkets that are springing up now. I found the one in Cannes so irresistible that Ben had to hold both my hands to keep me from forgetting that a hotel room is no place for a week's supply of groceries.

Our French Eat-In was a great success. The menu would be a bit much for one cook to tackle. With five people sharing the cooking, however, nobody felt unduly burdened and the result was, we agreed, the best French meal any of us had ever had in a home and far better than all but a few meals in great (expensive) restaurants.

Bon appetit!

France

Jane went slightly mad on the appetizer course. Emboldened by the fact that the paté could be made a leisurely week before the dinner, she decided to add "a few" hors d'oeuvres. When those she chose also turned out to be goodies that could be made ahead of time, she just went on adding others until we could have dined well on the first course alone. I've omitted a few of her hors d'oeuvres just so that your guests will have room for the rest of the dinner.

COUNTRY PÂTÉ

The pâté can be made well ahead of time. It can be kept refrigerated for several weeks if the surrounding fat is not removed. As a matter of fact, since it keeps so well, you may want to double the recipe and keep one pan for your family's refrigerator raiding.

¾ lb fresh pork fat
½ lb boneless veal
½ lb boneless pork shoulder
½ lb ham
¼ lb chicken livers
4 cloves garlic
2 oz heavy cream
2 eggs
¼ cup cognac
2 teaspoons salt (omit if your pork fat is salted)
1 teaspoon white pepper
¼ teaspoon allspice
¼ teaspoon cinnamon
¼ cup flour

1. Slice ⅓ of the pork fat in very thin slices.
2. Using a fine blade, grind half of the remainder of the pork fat with all of the veal and pork shoulder.
3. Line a loaf pan with the thin slices of pork fat, letting the long ends hang outside the pan.
4. Using the coarse blade of the grinder, grind the ham and the rest of the pork fat.
5. In an electric biender, purée the chicken livers with the garlic, cream, eggs and cognac. Gradually add and blend about ⅓ of the veal and pork mixture.
6. Now combine in a mixing bowl the mixture from the blender and all the other ground meat; the salt, pepper, allspice, cinnamon and flour. Mix thoroughly.
7. Fill the fat-lined bread pan with the mixture and fold the overhanging strips of pork fat over the top. Cover tightly with a double thickness of aluminum foil. Place the pan in a roasting pan into which you have poured two inches of water.
8. Bake at 400° for 3 hours, then remove the foil and bake for 20 minutes more.
9. Remove both pans from the oven. Leaving the loaf pan resting in the larger pan, place on top of the pâté a smaller pan. Fill this smaller pan with heavy objects to weight it down on the pâté. Keep the weights on until the pâté is completely cool.
10. Remove weights and refrigerate, covered.

France

ONIONS RIVIERA

2 lbs fresh small white onions, *peeled*
2 cups water
1 cup dry white wine
⅔ cup sugar
⅔ cup golden raisins
¼ cup tomato paste
¼ cup olive oil
3 tablespoons wine vinegar
salt and pepper to taste

1. Combine all ingredients and simmer for 45 minutes until onions are tender but still firm.
2. Refrigerate and serve cold.

CELERY PROVENÇALE

6 stalks celery
1 tablespoon salt
3 large ripe tomatoes
3 tablespoons olive oil
⅛ teaspoon salt
¼ teaspoon black pepper
2 cloves garlic, minced
2 tablespoons parsley, minced
6 anchovy filets
6 pitted black olives, cut in half

1. Cut the celery into 4-inch pieces and then split each piece into julienne strips.

2. Drop the celery into boiling water to which a tablespoon of salt has been added. Boil for 10 minutes. Drain.
3. Meanwhile, peel the tomatoes by cutting out the stem end, spearing each tomato on a long fork and holding it in boiling water for half a minute. The peel can then be removed easily with a paring knife or your fingers. Cut the tomatoes into small pieces, discarding the seeds.
4. Heat the olive oil in a pan and cook the tomatoes and garlic with salt and pepper to taste. When the tomatoes are reduced to a purée, add the parsley and 3 minced anchovies. Cook, stirring, one minute more.
5. Arrange the celery in a small serving dish. Pour the tomato purée over it and sprinkle a few drops of olive oil over the dish. Decorate with the remaining anchovies and the black olives.
6. Refrigerate until serving time.

MARINATED MUSHROOMS

2 lbs fresh small button mushrooms
1 and ½ tablespoons lemon juice
1 teaspoon salt

For Marinade

½ cup wine vinegar
½ cup olive oil
4 cloves garlic, crushed
2 sprigs parsley
1 bay leaf
5 peppercorns
12 coriander seeds

137

France

1. Stem and rinse mushrooms and put them in a saucepan with enough water to cover. Add the lemon juice and salt. Bring to a boil and then let simmer for 10 minutes.
2. Drain and place mushrooms in a bowl.
3. Combine the marinade ingredients in a saucepan. Bring to a boil, lower heat and let simmer for 30 minutes.
4. Pour the marinade over the mushrooms and refrigerate for at least 24 hours before serving.

TOMATOES VINAIGRETTE

> *3 large, ripe, firm tomatoes*
> *1 teaspoon salt*
> *2 tablespoons red wine vinegar*
> *6 tablespoons olive oil*
> *⅛ teaspoon thyme*
> *½ teaspoon dry mustard*
> *1 garlic clove, peeled*
> *¼ teaspoon black pepper*
> *3 tablespoons parsley, finely chopped*

The day before:

1. Mix the vinegar, oil, salt, thyme and mustard in a jar. Add the whole garlic clove and let the dressing stand for one day.
2. Slice the tomatoes with a very sharp knife into thin slices. Place the tomato slices, overlapping on a dish (a **long narrow glass hors d'oeuvres dish is ideal**) and cut down the center of all the slices.

138

3. Pour the dressing over the tomatoes and sprinkle with freshly ground pepper and minced parsley.
4. Refrigerate and serve cold.

EGGS IN ASPIC

5 *hard cooked eggs, cut in half*
5 *thin slices Virginia ham*
  tarragon leaves or scallions

For the Aspic

3 *cups chicken broth*
1 *cup tomato juice*
4 *envelopes unflavored gelatin*
1 *teaspoon sugar*
2 *egg whites*
2 *eggshells, crushed*
  salt and pepper
2 *tablespoons cognac*

1. Combine in a saucepan all of the aspic ingredients, except the cognac. Heat slowly, stirring constantly, until mixture boils. Remove pan from heat and add cognac.
2. Line a strainer with a piece of tightly woven cloth that has been rinsed in cold water and wrung out. Strain the aspic and chill it slightly but go on to the next step while the aspic is still liquid.
3. Pour a thin layer of aspic into 10 egg molds or custard dishes or cups of a muffin tin. Chill for 10 minutes.

139

4. Dip either tarragon leaves or the green part of scallions, cut to appropriate lengths, in the aspic and place two leaves in the bottom of each mold in a "V" shape.
5. Place an egg half in each mold, cut side up and top with an oval of ham. Fill the mold with aspic and chill until ready to serve.
6. The leftover aspic should be poured into a small flat pan and chilled. It can then be cut into shapes with a small cookie cutter and used, together with watercress, to garnish the eggs when they are unmolded.

Note: If the aspic starts to set before you've finished pouring it into the molds, it can be reheated slightly and chilled briefly before you use it.

BOUILLABAISSE

There are purists who will tell you that nothing can be called Bouillabaisse that is cooked out of the Marseilles area because the local fish are what give it its character. But even the great Savarin agrees with our feeling that it's the interesting mixture of fish that counts. You may not have available the esoteric fish of the Mediterranean, but we happen to be chauvinistic about the virtues of American shellfish. While we bow to both English and French oysters, European waters can't produce Maine lobsters, Maryland or Dungeness crabs, Louisiana shrimp or Long Island clams. Here's Marion's God-Bless-American-Shellfish Bouillabaisse.

Please don't be intimidated by the length of this recipe. There are actually three steps—preparing the velouté, the sauce and the fish. The first two can be done well ahead of time. In the morning, clean, cut and refrigerate the fish, make the velouté, make the sauce (which will only need the addition of some hot broth before serving) and cut the bread for the toast rounds. All this can be done at your leisure and there's very little work left in the actual cooking at dinner time.

To Prepare the Fish

> 10 *lobster tails*
> 1 *striped bass, about 3 lbs*
> 14 *clams, in shell*
> 1 *and ½ lbs small shrimp, shelled*
> 3 *whitings*
> *toasted bread rounds*

1. Clean, slice and refrigerate the fish early. Scrub the clams well, since they will be going into the soup with their shells.
2. Make the toasted bread rounds and cover tightly with plastic wrap.

France

To Prepare the Velouté

> 3 lbs fish heads, bones and trimmings, shrimp shells, codfish cheeks or lean fish
> 1 piece dried orange peel
> 1 onion, thinly sliced
> 1 bay leaf
> ½ teaspoon basil
> 1 tablespoon salt
> ½ teaspoon pepper
> 1 bottle white wine (a fifth)
> 2 tablespoons butter
> 3 tablespoons flour

1. Place all ingredients except the wine, butter and flour in a large pot and add enough water to cover. Cook over moderate heat, uncovered, for 40 minutes.
2. Strain and discard all the solid matter.
3. Return the strained liquid to the pot and add the wine. Cook down slowly until you have about 2 and ¾ quarts of stock.
4. Melt the butter in a large saucepan and add the flour, stirring constantly with a wire whisk. Add 2 cups of the fish bouillion gradually, stirring. Add the rest of the bouillion and mix well.
5. Refrigerate the velouté until ½ hour before serving time.

To Prepare the Sauce

½ cup canned pimento, minced
¼ teaspoon tabasco
2 medium potatoes, cooked and mashed
8 cloves garlic, minced
2 teaspoons thyme
½ cup olive oil

1. Mix all ingredients. Refrigerate until serving time.
2. Just before serving the sauce, add ¼ cup of the hot fish soup to it.
3. The sauce should be passed separately in a gravy boat.

To Put It All Together

1. A half hour before serving, place the lobster tails on the bottom of a tall, narrow kettle. Place the striped bass on top of the lobster and the clams in their shells on top of the bass.
2. Pour all the fish soup into the kettle.
3. When the mixture boils, add the shrimp and whiting and simmer for 15 minutes.
4. To serve, arrange the fish and shellfish attractively on a platter. Give each guest a bowl of soup. The sauce is spread on the toasted bread rounds which are then added to the soup. Each guest will help himself to fish from the platter and more of the sauce to put directly on the fish if desired.

France

RATATOUILLE

Behind that unpronounceable name is one of the world's great vegetable stews. It can be served either hot or cold. For this particular menu we like it cold, since it serves both as a vegetable and for the temperature contrast usually provided by a salad.

>   6 *baby eggplants or 1 medium eggplant*
>   6 *zucchini*
>   2 *large onions*
>   8 *tomatoes*
>   2 *green peppers*
>   3 *cloves of garlic*
>   ¼ *cup parsley, chopped*
>   1 *tablespoon salt*
>   ¼ *teaspoon pepper*
>   1 *cup olive oil*
>   5 *tablespoons capers*

1. Peel and slice the eggplant, zucchini, onions and green peppers. Mince the garlic.
2. Peel tomatoes by removing the stem with a knife and dipping each tomato on a long fork into boiling water for half a minute. The skin can then be peeled easily with your fingers. Chop the tomatoes.
3. Heat the olive oil in a heavy pot and sauté the onion until slightly golden. Add the garlic and cook for 5 minutes.
4. Add all the remaining ingredients, except the capers, and cook, covered, for one hour.
5. Five minutes before finished, add the capers and stir well.
6. Serve hot or refrigerate until needed.

FRENCH BREAD
(2 loaves)

> ½ cup scalded milk
> 1 cup boiling water
> 1 package yeast
> ¼ cup lukewarm water
> 1 and ½ tablespoons melted butter
> 1 tablespoon sugar

> { 4 cups sifted all-purpose flour
> 2 teaspoons salt
> 2 teaspoons sugar
> 1 egg white, beaten with 1 tablespoon cold water

1. Add 1 cup boiling water to ½ cup scalded milk—let liquid cool to lukewarm.
2. Sprinkle the yeast in ¼ cup lukewarm water. Cover and let stand in a warm, draft-free place for 7-8 minutes until it is bubbly. Transfer mixture to a larger bowl.
3. Add to the dissolved yeast, the scalded milk-water mixture, 1 and ½ tablespoons melted butter and 1 tablespoon sugar.
4. Add gradually ½ of the bracketed ingredients to the liquid. Blend thoroughly. (This first blending can be done by electric mixer.)
5. Add remainder of the bracketed ingredients and beat by hand. Do not knead.
6. Cover dough with a damp cloth and keep it out of drafts in a warm, protected place. (Elizabeth puts hers in a cupboard and says it works fine.) Let the dough

rise until doubled in bulk—about 1 and ½ to 2 hours.

7. Punch dough down with your fist, then fold the edges to the center and turn it upside down.

8. Turn out dough onto lightly floured board and divide into 2 oblong loaves.

9. With a rolling pin, roll out each half flat and then roll dough toward you with your hands—like a tight jelly roll.

10. Continue to roll toward you, while patting the roll and pressing outward with your hands and shaping the loaf. Roll gently back and forth to lengthen the roll and taper ends. Pinch each end closed.

11. Place 2 loaves diagonally on a greased baking sheet or an ungreased Teflon sheet.

12. Cut ¼ inch deep slits every 2 inches on top of loaf to form markings.

13. Set in warm place to rise to slightly less than double in bulk—about 1 hour.

14. Preheat oven to 400°.

15. Place pie tin filled with ½ inch boiling water on floor of oven. Brush tops of loaves with the beaten egg white and water mixture.

16. Bake bread for 15 minutes at 400°; reduce heat to 350° and bake 30 minutes more. About 5 minutes before the breads are finished, brush tops once more with the egg white mixture.

DEMI-MOUSSE WITH MERINGUES

To Prepare the Mousse

> ½ cup strong black coffee, very hot
> 1 tablespoon chicory
> pinch of salt
> 12 oz semisweet chocolate bits
> 8 egg yolks
> ¼ cup cognac

1. Put all ingredients, except the egg yolks and cognac, into the blender (being sure the coffee is very hot so that the chocolate will melt) and blend until smooth.
2. Add the egg yolks and cognac and blend again until the mixture is smooth.
3. Pour the mousse into a large glass bowl and refrigerate overnight.

To Prepare the Meringues

> 8 egg whites (room temperature)
> pinch of salt
> 1 tablespoon dark rum
> ½ teaspoon cream of tartar
> 2 cups sugar, sifted

1. Beat egg whites and salt in large bowl of electric mixer. When the whites are foamy, add the rum. Then add the

147

cream of tartar slowly through your sifter. Continue mixing until the egg whites form a peak when the beaters are raised.

2. Start adding the sugar, about ⅛ cup at a time, through your sifter. When all the sugar has been slowly added and the mixture is smooth (5 to 10 minutes of beating), it is ready to use.

3. Heat oven to 150°. Pour the meringue mixture into a pastry bag and shape the meringues into fans or triangles directly onto a Teflon baking pan or a regular cookie sheet lined with paper.

4. Bake slowly until the meringues are dry. This will take 2 to 3 hours. They are dry enough when they can be moved easily off the baking sheet and are of uniform consistency. (You'll have more meringues than you need so don't hesitate to taste a couple for doneness. You could cut the meringue recipe down but then what would you do with all those leftover egg whites? Any unused meringues can be frozen or stored in a cookie jar and make a fine companion for just plain old ice cream.)

5. To serve: Stick the meringues all around the edge of the bowl of mousse before serving.

CHINA

MENU

Spicy Shrimp

Hot and Sour Soup

Barbecued Spareribs

Dim Sum with Duck Sauce

Beef with Oyster Sauce

Rice or Noodles

Chinese Spinach Salad

Fresh Lichee Nuts

RICE WINE
JAPANESE PLUM WINE

When my children were young they once gave me a Monopoly game as a Christmas present. As they grew older, they grew more subtle and my kitchen gradually filled with gifts from which a suspicious soul might deduce that the givers anticipated some personal gain—like the year they gave me an electric grinder which by coincidence made their beloved Chicken Pojarski appear on the table more often than it did when I had to grind the chicken breasts in a manual grinder.

I'm not complaining, because it is to these hungry Magi that I owe my pleasure in Chinese cooking. A few years ago, I had been lamenting that I had been unable to take a course in Chinese cooking which I considered too esoteric to tackle unaided. My birthday present that year was three Chinese cookbooks accompanied by a note quoting back at me one of my favorite axioms, "If you can read, you can cook." I can recognize a thrown gauntlet as well as the next one. So I rolled up my sleeves, put on my reading glasses, plunged into the books, Chinatown, and the kitchen in that order and emerged a Chinese cook.

Many gourmets believe that the two great cuisines of the world are the French and Chinese. Luckily we don't have to choose between them, but, if one did, it would be significant that Chinese cooking has the enormous advantages of economy and health. It is a low cholesterol, low calorie cuisine and can be prepared with far less effort, time, and money than fine French food.

As with the Greeks, cooking is directly entwined with the philosophy of the culture. The writings of Confucius are replete with references to food. Confucius, incidentally, was a gourmet who refused to eat at all if the food was not pre-

150

pared exactly as he liked it and the table properly set. In order to meet the minimum standard, food must satisfy all the senses—taste, sight, touch, hearing and smell. Bamboo shoots, water chestnuts and rice noodles, for example, have very little taste; they are added to a dish to give a touch of crispness. Sizzling rice, which crackles when soup or a gravy dish is poured on top of it, illustrates how even the ears are involved in the enjoyment of food.

Economics and geography as well as philosophy have played their parts in the development of the cuisine. Have you ever wondered why Chinese food is always served in small bits? One legend is that during the Shun dynasty the emperor was so afraid of revolution that he had all the knives and the two-pronged forks in the kingdom collected, leaving each household with only one knife for use in the kitchen, thus making it necessary for food to be cut in the kitchen, rather than by the individual diner. It is far more likely, however, that it was the shortage of cooking fuel that was influential in setting the style. Timber was scarce in the plains and valleys of China and inaccessible in the mountains. Most people used dried twigs, laboriously gathered, for cooking. If fuel is scarce, people are not likely to develop a taste for pot roast, which needs long cooking. Instead, food was cut into small pieces before cooking so that it could be cooked rapidly without using more of the precious fuel than necessary. This famous "stir-fry" method of the Chinese has, incidentally, one great advantage for the contemporary cook. Ingredients can, in many cases, be chopped and/or mixed in advance, thereby cutting to a minimum the actual time needed to cook the dish—a great help when you don't know what time you'll want to serve dinner.

The Chinese don't normally eat bread with a meal. The person who would have the bread assignment is, therefore, free to undertake another dish. The traditional way to plan a meal is to have a dish for each two people plus rice or noodles. This menu will give you more than the requisite 5 courses needed to serve 10 people and has been planned so that you won't stumble over each other in the kitchen by having too many dishes which need last minute preparation.

SHOPPING SOURCES

This menu was carefully designed to avoid your needing special utensils. If you're fond of Chinese food, however, the basic utensils, wok, cleaver and steamer, are in the mail order catalogues of some of these sources. The one ingredient I was unable to find listed in any of the catalogues is hot pepper oil. I suspect most of the Chinese mail order houses do carry it even though it may not be listed. I have also included some non-Oriental sources of some ingredients and utensils in case you want to combine varying needs in one order.

FOUR SEAS INTERNATIONAL, P. O. Box 22, Williston Park, N. Y. 11596 or 345 Pennsylvania Avenue, Mineola, N. Y. 11501. Catalogue available. (Canned bamboo shoots, water chestnuts, fresh ginger root, cloud ears, tiger lily buds, Chinese mushrooms, oyster sauce, shrimp noodles, soy sauce, plum or duck sauce, sesame oil, Chinese teas, bean sauce.)

KAM SHING CO., 2246 S. Wentworth Avenue, Chicago, Illinois 60616. Catalogue available but 8¢ stamp must be enclosed with request. (Sesame oil, bean sauce, oyster sauce, plum sauce, mushrooms, bamboo shoots, water chestnuts, teas, noodles, won ton wrappers, lily flower, cloud ears, woks, cleavers.)

KWONG ON LUNG IMPORTERS, 680 North Spring Street, Los Angeles, California 90012. Catalogue available. (Bean sauce, plum sauce, canned bamboo shoots and water chestnuts, oyster sauce, won ton wrappers, sesame oil, fresh ginger root, teas, woks.)

OYAMA'S ORIENTAL FOOD SHOP, 1302 Amsterdam Avenue, New York, N. Y. 10027. Catalogue available. (Bean sauce, oyster sauce, plum sauce, soy sauce, canned bamboo shoots and water chestnuts, tree ears, tiger lily buds, chopsticks, Chinese soup spoons, woks, Chinese teas, sesame oil, shrimp noodles.)

PAPRIKAS WEISS, 1546 Second Avenue, New York, N. Y. 10028 Catalogue 25¢ (Chinese teas, cleaver, wok.)

H. ROTH & SON, 1577 First Avenue, New York, N. Y. 10028 or 968 Second Avenue, New York, N. Y. 10022. Catalogue available. (This is a continental house but does carry fresh ginger root and woks.)

China

The Chinese seldom eat dessert as such except as the end of a very elaborate banquet. The sweet taste for which we look forward to dessert is apt to come in the middle of a meal as it does in this menu. Melon is an excellent dessert but if you're really lucky you may be able to find when fresh lichee nuts are available in your area. The Florida crop is available in New York for about six weeks beginning in mid-June. India is now exporting the fresh nuts to England and the Indian crop as well as the Chinese may soon be available here. Lest you think me prejudiced when I tell you that the fresh lichee nut (as distinguished from either the canned or dried varieties) is one of the great taste experiences, I remind you that an eighth-century Chinese emperor met his downfall because he had relays of couriers traveling 1,000 miles on horseback to bring his favorite concubine fresh lichee nuts daily during the brief season. Try not to lose your kingdom in the process but it is worth an effort to find when and where you can buy fresh lichees in your area or whether you can get a sympathetic friend in a city with a Chinese population to airmail some to you.

SPICY SHRIMP

Strictly speaking, this dish should be cooked and served with the shrimp in the shell. I have some objection, however, to leaving all that lovely sauce on shells that are going to be discarded. I cheat a little and cook them unshelled; we also on this occasion cheated by serving them cold on toothpicks to accompany predinner drinks. You may want to do the same if your group prefers an American-style cocktail hour before dinner.

> 2 *lbs jumbo shrimp*
> ¼ *cup soy sauce*
> ½ *cup ketchup*
> ¼ *cup sherry*
> 1 *tablespoon hot pepper oil (optional)*
> 4 *scallions*
> 2 *tablespoons chopped fresh ginger**
> 6 *tablespoons oil*

1. Shell and devein shrimp.
2. Combine the soy sauce, ketchup, sherry and hot pepper oil in a bowl.
3. Chop the scallions, green part and all into ½ inch pieces.
4. Heat the oil in a wok or a large skillet. Add the shrimp and cook, stirring constantly for about 5 minutes, or until the shrimp have turned pink.
5. Add the scallions, the ginger and half of the liquid mixture and cook, stirring, for 3 minutes more.
6. Add the remainder of the liquid and cook 2 minutes more.
7. Serve either hot or cold.

*The ginger must be fresh ginger, not the powdered kind. Ginger can not only be found in Oriental food stores but in Indian and Mexican ones too. It will stay fresh for months if you peel it and put the chunks into a small jar filled with sherry in your refrigerator.

China

SOUR AND HOT SOUP

½ cup pork shreds
½ cup tree ears (*Measure these after soak-
    ing since they expand in water*)
4 dried Chinese mushrooms
16 tiger lily buds (golden needles)
½ cup canned bamboo shoots

⎧ ¼ cup wine vinegar
⎪ 1 teaspoon salt
⎪ 1 teaspoon sugar
⎨ 2 teaspoons soy sauce
⎪ ¼ teaspoon pepper
⎪ ½ teaspoon MSG
⎪ ¼ cup cornstarch
⎩ 6 tablespoons cold water

8 cups chicken broth
2 eggs, beaten
1 tablespoon sesame oil

1. Soak the mushrooms and tiger lily buds in warm water for half an hour. Wash them and cut the mushrooms into strips, discarding the hard stem. The tiger lily buds need only to be cut in half.
2. Soak the tree ears (also sometimes known as cloud ears or Chinese fungus) separately in warm water for half an hour. Wash and cut into small pieces.
3. Cut lean pork into thin strips, about ⅛ inch by 2 inches.
4. Cut the bamboo shoots into julienne strips. All these ingredients can be prepared ahead and put into the refrigerator until you are ready to make the soup.
5. Mix all the bracketed ingredients in a jar.

156

6. When you are ready to cook the soup, put the broth and the pork-vegetable mixture into a pot, bring to a boil and simmer 10 minutes.
7. Stir the bracketed mixture thoroughly since cornstarch has a bad habit of settling on the bottom. Add the mixture to the soup. Cook for 3-4 minutes more until the soup has thickened slightly.
8. Turn off the flame, pour in the beaten eggs, slowly, mixing the soup with a fork.
9. Add the sesame oil.

BARBECUED SPARERIBS

Some ingenious soul dreamed up this great substitute for the professional Chinese oven in which such delicacies as roast pork and barbecued spareribs are made. The method is simple: Remove all the racks from your oven except one and place that one as high in the oven as possible. Place on the bottom of the oven a roasting pan lined with aluminum foil and pour about an inch and a half of water in the pan. Using drapery hooks, hang the racks of spareribs from the oven rack as illustrated. The juice will drip into your aluminum-lined pan and the water in the pan will keep the ribs moist and tender.

This dish has an additional virtue as part of your Chinese dinner; it can be made the night before and reheated in the oven, which won't be in use for any other dish on the menu. One less last minute chore.

China

Have the butcher chop the fatty, bony top off the racks of ribs but leave the racks intact. This will enable you to cut the ribs into individual sections with no trouble.

> 2 *racks of spareribs*
> 3 *cloves garlic, minced*
> ½ *cup Chinese bean sauce*
> ½ *cup soy sauce*
> ½ *cup ketchup*
> 1 *tablespoon red food coloring*
> ¼ *cup sherry or rice wine*

1. Marinate the ribs in a mixture of all the other ingredients in a shallow pan for 2 hours at room temperature. Turn from time to time.
2. Arrange the oven as described above and hang the ribs. Turn the oven to 350° and bake for 45 minutes.
3. Refrigerate until an hour before you are ready to eat the ribs.
4. To serve, cut the rack into individual ribs and let stand at room temperature for ¾ hour.
5. Heat oven to 350° and reheat the ribs in a baking dish, covered lightly with aluminum foil, for 15 minutes.

DIM SUM

These little Chinese meat-filled dumplings are usually made in a steamer. If this dinner convinces you that you

158

Chinese roast pork can be made by the same method. Marinate pork strips about 2 inches wide (pork filet is excellent) in the same marinade and hang by a single hook to roast as illustrated on the left side of the drawing.

Improvised Steamer

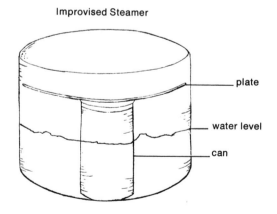

plate

water level

can

too can be a Chinese cook, the steamer is certainly something you will want to buy. In the meantime, however, you can improvise a steamer as follows: Take a very large pot and a tall empty can (a coffee can is fine) and remove both ends of the can. Place the can in the pot and pour water in the pot just about halfway up the side of the can. Your food to be steamed is placed on a plate set on top of the can. The plate should be a little smaller than the diameter of the pot so that steam from the boiling water can rise on all sides of the plate. (See illustration.)

In order to make all the dim sum at one time you will need to use two pots. Round up the old baby bottle sterilizing pots; they're a perfect size for this.

> *1 package wonton wrappers (or use recipe*
> *on p. 69)*
> *5 medium Chinese mushrooms*
> *3 scallions*
> *8 water chestnuts (canned)*
> *1 lb ground chicken*
> *3 tablespoons cornstarch*
> *1 teaspoon sesame oil*
> *1 teaspoon salt*
> *⅛ teaspoon pepper*
> *1 tablespoon sherry or rice wine*

1. Soak the mushrooms in warm water for half an hour. Rinse and remove and discard the hard stems.
2. If you have a food grinder, put the chicken, mushrooms, water chestnuts and scallions together through the grinder. If not, mince the mushrooms, water chestnuts and scallions as fine as possible and mix them with the chicken.

160

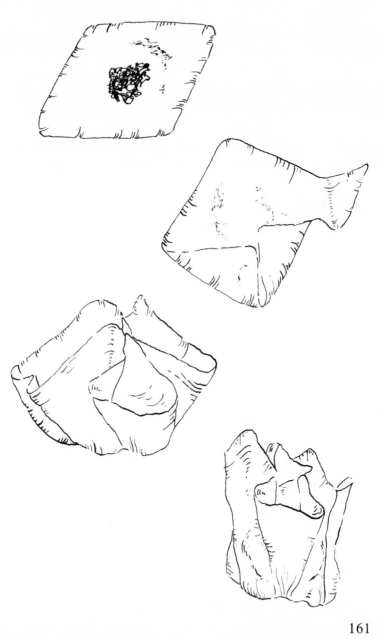

3. Add all other ingredients and mix well. Refrigerate until needed.
4. To make the dumplings, hold a wonton wrapper in the palm of your hand and put a tablespoon of filling in the center. Gather the edges of the wrapper around the filling and pinch tightly in the center. (See illustration.)
5. Place finished wonton on a lightly oiled plate, tapping it down on the plate a little so that the bottom is flat.
6. To cook, put the can and water in a pot as directed above. When the water is boiling, place the plate of wonton on top of the can and cover the pot. Steam for 20 minutes.
7. Serve with duck sauce.

DUCK SAUCE

It is possible to buy perfectly acceptable bottled duck sauce (also sometimes known as plum or sweet sauce) even in many non-Oriental foodstores. If you happen to be holding your dinner at a time of year when fruit is plentiful, you will find it rewarding to make your own.

> *enough plums, peaches and apricots to make 5 cups when pared, pitted and chopped*
> *½ cup red wine vinegar*
> *1 cup sugar*

1. Boil a pot of water. Holding each piece of fruit on a long fork, dip the fruit in the boiling water for 1 minute. This will make the skin easy to strip off.

162

2. Chop the fruit in small pieces, discarding the pits.
3. Mix the vinegar and sugar.
4. Put the fruit in a large pot, add the vinegar-sugar mixture and stir. Bring to a boil, stir, reduce heat and simmer for 1 and ½ hours, stirring occasionally.
5. Adjust seasoning if necessary. Serve cold.

BEEF WITH OYSTER SAUCE

This dish must be cooked at the last minute but if all the ingredients are prepared in advance (through Step 3), the actual cooking time is very short.

While this should properly be cooked in a wok, an electric frying pan is a good substitute. A nonelectric skillet can, of course, be used but it should be heated well before adding the oil.

3 lbs boneless sirloin, 1 and ½ inches thick
2 cloves garlic, minced
2 slices fresh ginger, crushed
3 scallions, chopped
12 water chestnuts

¼ cup sherry
¼ cup soy sauce
½ cup oyster sauce
1 cup chicken broth
2 tablespoons cornstarch
½ teaspoon salt
½ teaspoon sugar

3 tablespoons peanut oil

163

China

1. Put steak in freezer until cold but not frozen. Cut into slices ¼ inch thick.
2. Cut water chestnuts into 4 slices.
3. Mix bracketed ingredients together.
4. Heat electric frying pan to highest heat. Add oil.
5. When oil is hot, add ginger and garlic and cook briefly, stirring, until brown.
6. Add steak and cook quickly, turning pieces until outside is brown. Remove steak from pan.
7. Add the scallions and water chestnuts to the pan and cook for 1 minute. Remove with a slotted spoon and put aside with the beef.
8. Stir the bracketed mixture again to dissolve the cornstarch and pour the mixture into the pan. Cook, stirring, until sauce is hot and thick.
9. Return beef, scallions and water chestnuts to pan and heat briefly in gravy before serving.

CHINESE SPINACH SALAD

1 lb fresh spinach
1 and ½ teaspoons salt
5 tablespoons sesame oil
3 tablespoons cooked ham, minced
3 tablespoons roasted peanuts, crushed

1. Wash the spinach and discard the hard stems. Chop the spinach into convenient salad pieces. Refrigerate.
2. Just before serving, add all the other ingredients and mix well.

164

RICE OR NOODLES

To keep down the traffic in the kitchen, either make rice in your usual fashion to serve at the same time the beef is served or, while you're doing your Chinese marketing, see if you can pick up a package of shrimp noodles. These are delicately flavored noodles which cook in just 3 minutes in boiling water. You'll find them in boxes in the dried noodle department of a Chinese grocery, or you can get them through one of the mail order sources suggested.

COLONIAL VIRGINIA

MENU

Virginia Mint Juleps

Peanut Soup

Black Bean Soup

Roast Chicken

Beets Greens

Apricot-Pear Conserve

Spoon Bread

Skillet Bread

Syllabub

I used to be very self-conscious about going through customs when returning to the United States from abroad—not, I hasten to assure you because I was smuggling in undeclared goodies. But I do have a habit of bringing back things that clearly place me in the customs agents' minds as an oddball—bottles of seasoning from Switzerland, spinach lasagna noodles from Italy, etc. Thanks to Thomas Jefferson, I'm no longer even apologetic about my eccentricity. Jefferson went so far as to smuggle rice out of the Piedmont while on a diplomatic mission at a time when Piedmont law made taking the rice out of the country a crime punishable by death. This may have been Jefferson's most daring importation of food into the country, but it was by no means his only one.

He was an eager farmer and an even more eager gourmet. He imported such disparate things as French wine, Calcutta hogs and what was probably the first waffle iron brought into the States. He is credited with being the first to serve spaghetti at a formal dinner, to introduce French fried potatoes as an accompaniment to beefsteak, to serve ice cream and to propagandize for the edibility of the tomato, which had theretofore been raised primarily for its ornamental value.

It is fitting that Columbus' voyages, which did not produce the spices from India for which they were undertaken, did serve to introduce dozens of new foods to the European world—potatoes, yams, tomatoes, peanuts, green peppers, chocolate, vanilla, chili, guava, avocados, pineapples, beans, squash, corn, turkey and wild rice, to name but a few.

The early settlers perforce had to learn to use the strange foods of the new world, though it took some time for some of the best to be regarded as they merited. Lobster, though abundant, for example, was not really considered food fit for fashionable folk until the middle of the nineteenth century. The Indians taught the settlers to use corn, without which they often might not have survived. It was frequently used as the basis for breads such as pone, a mixture of corn flour and water shaped into flat cakes and baked in an oven on wooden platters or in the ashes of a hearthfire (ashcake) or baked on a hoe over an open fire (hoecake).

To a very large extent the cooking was English where that was possible. The first cookbook published in the Colonies in 1742, the **Williamsburg Cookbook,** was really an adaptation of an English cookbook from which the American editor deleted the recipes calling for ingredients not available in this country. Most other eighteenth-century cookbooks were likewise basically English, ignoring American foods. The first to use at least some indigenous recipes was a book by Amelia Simmons in 1796 which included such un-English items as watermelon rind and johnnycake, which is probably a perversion of its original name, journey cake.

Our Colonial Virginia dinner reflects both the English and the American influence. There are no hors d'oeuvres, since they were not part of the English cooking of the century and certainly not a feature of pioneer cooking. Soup, on the other hand, had an important role. If you think of the twentieth century as the era of food concentrates, try reading one of the recipes in the Williamsburg book for "pocket soup" or "cake soup," which literally was a strong solid made from veal stock which could be carried in the pocket or saddlebag and reconstituted with water over an open fire.

We've given you two recipes for soup. We made both since we were afraid the peanut soup might be appreciated more for its historical than gustatory value. We were wrong; everybody loved it. You can ring a change on the black bean soup if you like by substituting black-eyed peas— unusual and delicious.

The rest of the meal is a mixture of the English and American tastes of the day, but perhaps our greatest discovery was the Virginia mint julep which bears no resemblance to any other mint julep you've tasted, other than the fact that it's lethal. But what a way to go!

SHOPPING SOURCES

The only unusual ingredient needed for this dinner is fresh ginger root which can be bought in Chinese, Japanese or Mexican food stores or ordered by mail from:

FOUR SEAS INTERNATIONAL, P. O. Box 22, Williston Park, N. Y. 11596 or 345 Pennsylvania Avenue, Mineola, New York 11501.

KWONG ON LUNG IMPORTERS, 680 North Spring Street, Los Angeles, California 90012.

H. ROTH & SON, 1577 First Avenue, New York, N. Y. 10028 or 968 Second Avenue, New York, N. Y. 10022.

Colonial Virginia

VIRGINIA MINT JULEP

fresh mint leaves
crushed ice
1 part brandy, 1 part cognac, mixed together

1. Crush a few mint leaves in the bottom of each glass with the back of a spoon.
2. Fill the glass with crushed ice.
3. Pour the mixed brandies over the ice.
4. Decorate with a sprig of mint.

VIRGINIA PEANUT SOUP

1 and ½ cups roasted peanuts
9 cups beef broth
1 and ½ cups milk
1 and ½ cups light sweet cream
2 teaspoons chili powder
1 and ½ teaspoons salt
2 cucumbers, thinly sliced

1. Blend peanuts with 3 cups of the broth in the blender at high speed for 1 minute. Pour into a saucepan and add all remaining ingredients except the cucumbers.
2. Bring to a boil, reduce heat, cover and simmer for 15 minutes. Refrigerate.
3. Serve cold with slices of cucumber floating in each bowl.

172

BLACK BEAN SOUP

3 *cups dried black beans*
1 *ham hock*
3 *onions, chopped*
3 *carrots, chopped*
4 *stalks celery, chopped*
8 *sprigs parsley*
2 *tablespoons salt*
½ *teaspoon pepper*
⅛ *teaspoon mace*
¼ *teaspoon thyme*
3 *bay leaves*
2 *teaspoons dry mustard*
2 *tablespoons Worcestershire Sauce*
6 *oz sherry*
10 *thin slices of lemon*

1. Wash the beans and put in a large kettle with 3 quarts of water. Add all the ingredients except the sherry and lemon slices. Bring to a boil, cover and reduce heat and simmer for 2 and ½ hours. Discard the ham hock.
2. Put the soup, a small quantity at a time, through your blender. Then strain all the soup through a strainer into another pot, pressing down on the beans with the back of a wooden spoon to get all the liquid out.
3. When you are ready to reheat the soup, add the sherry. Garnish each bowl with a slice of lemon.

ROAST CHICKEN

If you want to save a step, you can use undiluted condensed chicken broth as the stock for the sauce. Unless time is of the essence, however, we recommend making the

173

chicken stock according to the directions at the end of the recipe.

Roast Chicken

> 5 lb roasting chicken
> ¼ lb butter
> 1 cup sherry
> 1 lemon
> salt and pepper

1. Cut the lemon in half and use one half to rub the inside and outside of the chicken. Sprinkle salt and pepper generously inside the cavity and over the outside of the chicken. Put the remaining half of the lemon in the cavity.
2. Heat oven to 350°. Melt the butter in the roasting pan and brush butter over the outside of the chicken.
3. Put the chicken in the roasting pan and bake for ½ hour.
4. Pour the sherry over the chicken and bake for another 1½ hours, basting the chicken frequently with the sherry and pan drippings.
5. Remove the chicken from the bones and cut it into large pieces. Don't remove the skin.

Roast Chicken Sauce

> 6 tablespoons butter
> 3 tablespoons flour
> 3 cups chicken stock
> 2 egg yolks, beaten
> 1 pint heavy sweet cream
> ½ cup sherry
>   pinch of nutmeg
>   salt and pepper

1. Melt 4 tablespoons of the butter and add the flour gradually. Stir with a wire whisk over low heat until smooth.
2. Add the chicken stock gradually, stirring until smooth. Cook over low heat for 15 minutes, stirring frequently with the whisk.
3. Pour the sauce over the chicken pieces and place in a very low oven to keep warm.
4. Melt the remaining 2 tablespoons of butter in the top of a double boiler.
5. Meanwhile, beat the egg yolks in a bowl with a wire whisk and add the cream gradually. Add this mixture to the melted butter, add the nutmeg and continue cooking in the double boiler, stirring frequently until the sauce is slightly thickened.
6. Add the sherry and mix. Taste for seasoning and add some salt and pepper if needed. Continue to heat in the double boiler until the sauce is hot.
7. Pour the sauce over the chicken, blending it with the stock sauce. The chicken can be served shortcake style, if you wish, over the skillet bread.

Colonial Virginia

To Make Chicken Stock

> *chicken neck, heart, liver, gizzard and*
>   *wings*
> ½ *bunch celery cut in large pieces*
> 1 *large onion, stuck with 4 cloves*
> 12 *peppercorns*
> 1 *quart water*

1. Put all ingredients in a saucepan, bring to a boil, lower heat, cover pan and simmer for 2 hours.
2. Strain and discard all solids.
3. Reserve 3 cups of the stock to use in the sauce.

BEET GREENS

> 2 *and* ½ *lbs beet greens*
> 1 *tablespoon salt*
> 5 *tablespoons melted butter*
>   *salt and pepper to taste*

1. Wash each leaf, cutting off the pink stem as close to the leaf as possible.
2. Put about 1 inch of water in the bottom of a large pot. Bring the water to a fast boil, add the tablespoon of salt and the greens and cover the pot tightly.
3. Simmer gently for 15-20 minutes or until greens are just tender, not wilted.
4. Drain the greens and dress with the melted butter. Add salt and pepper.

APRICOT-PEAR CONSERVE

4 large pears
1 cup dried apricots
1 inch piece of ginger root
½ lemon
½ cup golden raisins
2 tablespoons brandy

The Night Before

1. Put the brandy and raisins in a saucepan and heat over very low heat for a few minutes until the raisins become plump. Remove from heat.
2. Mix the apricots, raisins and brandy together and store in refrigerator in a covered jar.
3. Wash and core pears and cut into small pieces. Measure the cut pears in a measuring cup and place in a covered dish with an equal amount of sugar. Refrigerate.

The Next Day

1. Grate the peeled ginger root. Squeeze the lemon and grate the rind.
2. Add the ginger, lemon juice, lemon rind and the apricot-brandy mix to the pears. Mix well and put it all into a covered baking dish.
3. Bake at 325° for 3 hours.
4. The conserve can be served hot from the oven or at room temperature.

177

Colonial Virginia

SPOON BREAD

> 1 and ½ cups boiling water
> 1 cup corn meal
> 1 egg, beaten
> 1 teaspoon butter
> 1 cup buttermilk
> 1 teaspoon baking soda
> 1 teaspoon salt
> ½ cup milk

1. Pour boiling water over corn meal and let the mixture cool.
2. Add all remaining ingredients except the ½ cup of milk. Mix well and pour batter into greased square 8 or 9-inch pan.
3. Bake at 375° for 45 minutes. Every 10 minutes or so during baking, dribble a couple of teaspoons of the milk over the surface of the bread. This will keep it soft.

SKILLET BREAD

Traditionally a skillet bread is made over an open fire. Since this is slightly impractical for us apartment dwellers, we made ours in the oven, which we suspect probably produces more predictable results anyway. A 10-inch Corning ware or cast-iron skillet is perfect. If you have neither available to you, use the nearest equivalent that has a cover.

½ cup sifted flour
2 and ½ teaspoons baking powder
1 teaspoon salt
1 tablespoon sugar
1 and ½ cups corn meal
1 egg
¾ cup milk
2 tablespoons melted butter

1. Sift the flour, baking powder, salt and sugar together. Add the cornmeal.
2. In another bowl, beat the egg and add the milk and melted butter. Mix and then pour the mixture into the bowl of dry ingredients. Mix well.
3. Set the oven to 425°. Grease the bottom and sides of the skillet generously with butter and place the skillet in the oven to heat the butter.
4. Pour the batter into the hot skillet, cover the skillet and bake for 25 minutes.

SYLLABUB

1 and ½ fresh lemons
2 tablespoons brandy
¾ cup confectioners' sugar
2 and ½ cups heavy sweet cream
¾ cup white wine

1. Peel one lemon with a vegetable peeler to remove the peel with as little pulp as possible. Extract the juice from

the 1 and ½ lemons. Add the brandy to the juice and lemon peel and let the mixture stand overnight.

2. Remove and reserve the lemon peel. Add the sugar to the juice-brandy mixture and stir until it is dissolved.
3. Cut the rind in julienne pieces and blanch in hot water for 1 minute. Drain and reserve rind.
4. Whip the cream until it stands in peaks. Continue to whip adding the sugar mixture gradually and then the wine. Beat until the mixture is firm. Refrigerate until ready to use.
5. To serve, put the syllabub into individual sherbet glasses and top each serving with a few strips of lemon rind.

RUSSIA

Flavored Vodkas

Eggplant Caviar

Pickled Grapes

Blini Caviar

Chicken Pojarski

Russian Red Cabbage

Pumpernickel Rolls

Cheese Cake

Fruit Kissel

There are ten distinct Russian cuisines and we won't attempt a description of them, since you have only one Russian dinner to prepare and you might very well be tempted to try all ten styles before moving on to another country. The cooking styles are as varied as Russia's vast territory and its history might suggest—ranging from cuisines reminiscent of the Middle East, Germany and Scandinavia to the French influence stemming from the eighteenth and nineteenth centuries when everything French was held in high esteem by people of fashion.

Apart from all the outside influences, there is much that is uniquely Russian. Perhaps the most fascinating is the zakuska (sometimes spelled zakusky or zakuski) table which was in many households set up at all times for travelers or visitors—a welcome kind of hospitality in a country where distances were long between towns, transportation slow and weather severe. The zakuska table consisted of dozens of cold dishes with hot ones, too, becoming customary in the early part of the twentieth century. In addition to serving as a kind of free lunch **extraordinaire,** zakuska were frequently eaten before or after the theater or merely as a prelude to a meal.

We did not undertake the zakuska for the same reason that we did not start with a Russian soup—doubts about the quantity of food our effete American tummies could handle at one meal. (Russian borscht, laden with vegetables and meat and served with dumplings in the soup or pirozhki— meat, cheese or vegetable stuffed pastries—on the side is a meal by itself and would have left the other four cooks with no market for their wares.) The blini, which were our first course, however, need no apology. Indeed they were

182

one of our great discoveries in the course of the Eat-In and have since appeared as the mainstay of very special Sunday brunch occasions.

The Chicken Pojarski, named for the innkeeper who invented the dish, was originally designed to be made with partridge or other wild fowl. Chicken became the more popular ingredient as society became more urbanized and wild fowl less accessible. If you happen to live in a good hunting area, you might want to try it the original way.

Eat Russian with Love!

SHOPPING SOURCES

The only ingredient you may have trouble finding is buckwheat flour. A health food store may have it if your regular grocer doesn't. You may also want to try Russian tea. Both the flour and the tea are available from:

AMERICAN TEA, COFFEE AND SPICE COMPANY, 1511 Champa Street, Denver, Colorado 80202. Catalogue available.

PAPRIKAS WEISS, 1546 Second Avenue, New York, N. Y. 10028. Catalogue 25¢.

H. ROTH & SON, 1755 First Avenue, New York, N. Y. 10028 or 968 Second Avenue, New York, N. Y. 10022. Catalogue available.

Russia

FLAVORED VODKA

Part of the popularity of vodka in the United States stems, I am sure, from the fact that many people like the effect of liquor rather than the flavor. Vodka, having no distinctive taste, is an ideal drink for people who think orange juice tastes better than scotch. While the Bloody Mary and the Screwdriver are non-Russian in origin, flavored vodka does have a place in authentic Russian drinking. If you make all four of the suggested flavored vodkas, you'll have 2 quarts of potent beverage. We guarantee it will be finished either during cocktail time or by the lucky people who get to do the dishes.

1. Remove all the white flesh from the peel of a lemon. Soak the lemon peel in a pint of vodka for 4 hours. Remove the peel.
2. Remove the cardboard tag from one good tea bag and soak the tea bag in a pint of vodka for 2 hours. Remove the tea bag.
3. Add 2 teaspoons of peppercorns to a pint of vodka. Strain after 2 hours.
4. Soak 2 dozen halved, pitted, dark sweet cherries (canned will do) in 1 pint of vodka for 3 hours. For authenticity, the cherries should probably be discarded before serving the vodka, but you may prefer to serve a cherry half in each drink.

EGGPLANT CAVIAR

This dish can be prepared in a blender instead of using a food grinder. It will produce "caviar" of smoother texture.

184

If a blender is used, the peeled eggplant and the peppers should be cut in chunks and blended together with all the other ingredients.

The eggplant can be served on small pumpernickel slices. Since our menu for the evening included pumpernickel rolls, we served the eggplant with sesame crackers.

> 2 *medium eggplants*
> ½ *cup onion, minced*
> ¼ *cup olive oil*
> ½ *cup lemon juice*
> 1 *tablespoon salt*
> 2 *teaspoons sugar*
> ½ *teaspoon pepper*
> 1 *green pepper and 1 red pepper*

1. Bake eggplants in a 475° oven for 15 minutes by which time the skin will have turned dark brown. Cool and peel the eggplants.
2. Run the eggplants and the red and green peppers through a food grinder. Add remaining ingredients, mix and refrigerate.

PICKLED GRAPES

These should be made a week before they are to be used. They can be kept in the refrigerator for several months, however, if you happen to have any left over. They are excellent served with vodka.

Russia

1 lb seedless grapes, stripped from stems
6 oz wine vinegar
6 oz water
¾ teaspoon salt
5 tablespoons sugar
3 peppercorns
1 clove

1. Wash the grapes and put them in a jar.
2. Put all other ingredients in a saucepan and bring to a boil. Remove from heat, cool and pour the liquid over the grapes.
3. Cover jar and refrigerate.

BLINI WITH CAVIAR

Since the blini batter must be started about 6 hours before serving time, you may hit a logistics problem. Transporting any yeast batter from one house to another presents draft hazards. If the person responsible for the blini doesn't live close enough to the evening's hostess to enable her to pop in and mix the batter in the hostess' kitchen, a good-natured hostess (and we, happily, have no other kind) can do the preliminary batter mixing. The person responsible for the blini can arrive a trifle early—toward the end of the 2 hour resting period—and finish her job while the eggplant caviar and flavored vodkas are being consumed.

For the Blini

> ½ cup warm water
> 2 packages dry yeast
> 1 teaspoon sugar
> 2 cups white flour
> ½ cup buckwheat flour
> 2 cups milk
> 3 eggs
> ½ teaspoon salt
> ¼ lb sweet butter
> 3 tablespoons sour cream

For the Filling

> 12 oz red or black caviar
> 1 pint sour cream

1. Discard 2 scant teaspoons of yeast from one of the yeast packages. Sprinkle the remaining yeast and the sugar over the warm water. Cover the mixture and let it stand in a warm, draft-free place for 7-8 minutes until the mixture has bubbled. Meanwhile, warm 1 cup of the milk.
2. Pour the white flour and half of the buckwheat flour into a large mixing bowl. Make a well in the center and pour in the cup of warm milk and the yeast mixture. Stir with a large wooden spoon until the mixture is smooth.
3. Cover the bowl with a cloth and let it stand in a warm place for 3 hours; it will have doubled in volume by that time.

187

4. Add the remaining buckwheat flour and mix well. Recover the bowl with the cloth and let it stand for 2 more hours.

5. Just before the two-hour period is up, warm the remaining cup of milk and separate the eggs. Beat the yolks lightly in one bowl. In another, beat the whites until they are stiff. Melt the butter.

6. At the end of the two-hour resting period, stir the batter again and mix in the cup of warm milk, the egg yolks, 3 tablespoons of the melted butter, the sour cream and salt. Then fold the egg whites into the batter. Cover the batter with a towel and let it rest for half an hour.

7. When you are ready to cook the blini, heat the oven to 200° so that the finished blini can be kept warm while others are cooking. We found a Teflon lined electric frying pan perfect for the cooking. You can, however, use any large skillet or grill. Brush the pan lightly with melted butter and heat the pan.

8. Using a ladle that holds 3 to 4 tablespoons, pour the pancake mixture so as to make individual pancakes about 4 inches in diameter. Cook for about 2 minutes until the bottoms of the pancakes are light brown. Turn and brush the cooked tops with melted butter.

9. When the bottoms have cooked for about 2 minutes, remove with a spatula and keep the blini warm in the oven while you cook the remaining pancakes. Be sure to brush the pan lightly with melted butter before each new batch.

10. To serve the pancakes, put the caviar and sour cream in separate bowls. Each guest will take a pancake and add the filling to his own taste. The pancake can then be rolled up and eaten either with a fork or with the fingers.

CHICKEN POJARSKI

Many years ago I was somewhat offended to learn that my Chicken Pojarski was admiringly known among Jonny's college classmates as "those great chickenburgers." I was appeased when I heard a captain in London's elegant Les Ambassadeurs describe them to an inquiring guest the same way.

It may be more authentically Russian to serve these with a plain butter or mushroom sauce but we love the paprika sauce and so did the rest of the Eat-In members.

6 *large chicken breasts, skinned and boned*
1 *teaspoon salt*
¼ *teaspoon pepper*
1 *and ½ sticks sweet butter*
¾ *cup sifted flour*
2 *teaspoons oil*
2 *eggs, beaten*
2 *tablespoons cold water*
2 *cups fresh bread crumbs (see Step 2)*

1. Melt 6 tablespoons of the butter and allow it to cool while you grind the chicken breasts. Mix the ground chicken, melted butter, salt and pepper in a bowl and refrigerate for an hour.
2. Remove the crusts from about 7 slices of white bread and make the crumbs in your blender.
3. Put the flour on a piece of aluminum foil. Mix the eggs, water and oil in a plate. Pour the bread crumbs on another piece of foil.
4. Remove the chicken mixture from the refrigerator and

189

form it into smallish patties, about ¾ inch thick. (You should have 20 patties.)

5. Coat the patties on both sides with the flour, then the egg mixture and then the bread crumbs. Refrigerate for at least an hour (though longer won't hurt them a bit).

6. To cook, heat the remaining butter in a large skillet (350° in an electric pan) and cook patties about 10 minutes on each side. Serve with butter or mushroom sauce or with the following paprika sauce.

Paprika Sauce

> 2 *tablespoons butter*
> ¼ *cup onion, minced*
> 1 *tablespoon flour*
> 2 *teaspoons paprika*
> ½ *cup chicken broth*
> ½ *cup heavy cream*
> 1 *teaspoon brandy*
> 2 *teaspoons lemon juice*
> ¼ *cup sour cream*

1. Melt one tablespoon of the butter and sauté the onion until light golden.

2. Sprinkle the paprika and flour over the onions and mix gently. Add the chicken broth and cook, stirring constantly for about 4 minutes before adding the heavy sweet cream. Bring just to a boil and remove from the heat.

3. Add the brandy and lemon juice and strain the sauce through a strainer. (At this point you can, if you wish, put the sauce aside or in the refrigerator and add the

remaining ingredients and complete the cooking just before serving time.)

4. Add the remaining tablespoon of butter and the sour cream to the sauce and heat, stirring from time to time. Do not let the sauce boil.
5. Pass the sauce in a gravy boat to be spooned over the chicken patties.

If you prefer a more traditional sauce, here it is:

Mushroom Sauce

> ½ lb fresh mushrooms, chopped
> 1 onion, chopped
> 3 tablespoons butter
> 1 teaspoon flour
> 1 cup sour cream
>   salt and pepper

1. Brown onions lightly in the butter.
2. Add the mushrooms and cook over low heat for 20 minutes. Add flour and salt and pepper to taste.
3. Just before serving add the sour cream and reheat the sauce but do not let it boil.

RUSSIAN RED CABBAGE

> 2 medium red cabbages
> 2 teaspoons salt
> 4 tablespoons butter
> 2 large cooking apples, peeled and diced
> ¼ teaspoon pepper
> 2 tablespoons sugar
> ¼ cup lemon juice
> 2 tablespoons vinegar

191

Russia

1. Wash and shred the cabbages and place in a large pot.
2. Pour enough boiling water over the cabbage to cover it completely. Put the cover on the pot and let it stand for 20 minutes.
3. Drain in a colander and melt the butter in the same pot. When the butter is melted, return the drained cabbage to the pot, add the salt and stir well.
4. Add the apple to the cabbage mixture, cover the pot and cook slowly for half an hour, stirring occasionally.
5. Remove the pot from the stove and add the pepper, sugar, lemon juice and vinegar. Taste and adjust the seasoning if necessary.

RUSSIAN PUMPERNICKEL ROLLS

1 cup water
1 cup milk
¼ cup molasses
2 tablespoons butter
1 package yeast
1 teaspoon salt
2 and ½ cups rye flour
2 and ½ cups whole wheat flour

1. Place water, milk, molasses and butter in a saucepan. Heat, stirring, until butter melts. Do not boil.
2. While this is heating, mix the yeast and salt together.
3. Mix the 2 flours together.
4. Add the warm liquid to the yeast-salt mixture. Add 1 and ½ cups of the flour and beat for about 2 minutes. Add another ½ cup of flour and beat for 2 more min-

utes. Add the remaining flour and beat until the mixture forms a sticky ball.

5. Remove the dough to a lightly floured board and knead hard for 15 minutes, using more flour for the board if necessary.

6. Place the dough in a deep greased bowl, turning so that all sides of the dough ball are slightly oiled. Cover bowl with a tea towel and let stand in a warm place until the dough doubles in bulk—about 2 hours.

7. Punch the dough down. Cover it and let it rest for 10 minutes. Then turn the dough out on a floured board and divide it into 36 small round pieces.

8. Place the rolls on a greased baking sheet, cover them with the towel again and let them stand in a warm place for 1 more hour.

9. Heat oven to 325° and bake the rolls on the center rack for 20-30 minutes.

VATRUSHKA

(Russian Cheese Cake)

For the Pastry

> 2 and ½ cups sifted all purpose flour
> ¾ cup sugar
> ½ teaspoon salt
> ¼ lb plus 2 tablespoons salted butter
> 2 eggs

Russia

1. Sift the flour, sugar and salt together into a large bowl.
2. Break the butter into bits into the bowl and work the butter into the flour mixture with your fingers.
3. Add the eggs and blend them into the mixture.
4. Shape the mixture into a ball and knead on a lightly floured board just until the ingredients are well blended. Roll the dough into a circle about ⅜ inch thick.
5. Heat the oven to 350°. Butter the bottom and sides of a round layer cake pan. Place the dough into the pan, covering the sides and the bottom. Let the dough project all the way up the sides of the pan and a bit above the edge, since it shrinks a little in baking.
6. Bake the empty crust for 5 minutes. Then remove it and add the filling.

For the Filling

½ *lb cream cheese*
½ *cup sugar*
4 *eggs*
¼ *cup seedless raisins*
4 *dried apricots, diced*
¼ *cup vodka*

1. Let the cream cheese stand at room temperature until soft. With an electric mixer, blend the sugar into the cheese.
2. Add the eggs and vodka and mix well.
3. Mix the raisins and apricot bits in with a spoon or spatula.
4. Pour the filling into the crust and bake at 350° for 30 minutes.

194

FRUIT KISSEL

Kissel is a tart pudding made with berries or cherries. Because the winter is such an appropriate season for a Russian dinner, I'm assuming that fresh fruit won't be practical and the recipe is therefore adjusted to the use of frozen fruit. Russians usually serve kissel by passing light sweet cream to pour over the individual portions. Straight sweet cream is unusual to the American palate and, if you want to cheat a bit, you might make a bowl of whipped cream available.

> 3 *12-oz packages of frozen raspberries, strawberries, blueberries or cherries. (Be sure you get the kind packaged in syrup.)*
> 1 *cup water*
> 2 *tablespoons and 2 teaspoons cornstarch*
> *sugar (optional)*
> *sweet cream or whipped cream for serving*

1. Put the fruit and the cup of water in a large enamel or glass pot. Bring to a boil, reduce heat and simmer gently until the fruit is very soft.
2. Strain through a fine sieve and discard pits or seeds. Taste and add a little sugar if absolutely necessary. Pour the mixture back into the pot.
3. Mix the cornstarch in ¼ cup of cold water and add it to the fruit mixture. Bring the mixture to a boil again and boil for 2 minutes, stirring constantly.
4. Remove the kissel from the stove and pour it into a

195

serving bowl. Cover the top of the bowl immediately with aluminum foil. Let the kissel stand until it has reached room temperature. It can then be refrigerated, still covered, until serving time.

MIDDLE EAST

MENU

Cocktails

Falafel

Arab Bread

Stuffed Bass

Stewed Carrots

Cheese-Stuffed Peppers

Chocolate Hazelnut Cake

CARMEL CHABLIS ISRAEL

As is obvious from the title of this chapter, indecision hit us here. We couldn't quite agree on which of the countries of the Middle East to nominate for our dinner, so we decided to give ourselves the leeway of all the Mid-East countries and let the national boundary lines fall where they might. Actually, of course, while there are individual specialties in each country, there are great basic similarities in the cuisines of Lebanon, Egypt, Syria, Iraq, Saudi Arabia, Iran and Israel. Lamb is the most popular meat—usually barbecued or roasted; whole or in shish-kebab style. Pork is used very little since it is contrary to the religious traditions of both the Jews and the Muslims. Beef, kid and camel are utilized in about that order of frequency. Meat stews cooked with fruit rather than vegetables are most frequently found in Persia, but this kind of combination occurs in the other Middle East countries as well.

A heavy use of eggplant, chick peas, lentils, stuffed grape leaves, nuts, olives and olive oil, yogurt and burghul is common to all the countries comprising the area. Yogurt, which has only recently been discovered by diet conscious Americans, is usually placed on the table to be used as an accompaniment to anything from salad to bread to vegetables and, additionally, is frequently used as a cooking liquid. Burghul, a very fine boiled and drained wheat, appears in salads, as a thickening agent in cooking, in baking, and as a pilau instead of rice.

While the indigenous cuisine of Israel is very like that of her neighbors, the influx of Jews from other parts of the world during this century has introduced into Israel foods of the Near and Far East, North Africa and Central Europe. These mingle with the traditional Middle Eastern foods and

198

with a "Sabra" or native cuisine which is being deliberately and scientifically developed to best utilize the ingredients most available in Israel.

Like India, the Middle East was a prime source of spices with all the concommitant disadvantages and advantages for their countries of origin. A Portuguese traveler once wrote, ". . . the clove, though a creation of God, is actually an apple of discord and responsible for more afflictions than gold." Spices were a compact cargo, sometimes selling in Europe for as much as an equivalent weight of pure gold. Small wonder that for so profitable a cargo, European shippers were willing to send ten ships on a hazardous journey, knowing that if only one returned, the profits would be sufficient to absorb the loss of the other nine. While not in the same profit category as spices, sugar and melons were also introduced to Europe via the Middle East. Notwithstanding the availability of many of the same spices, Middle Eastern cooking does not rely on heavy seasoning or spicy mixtures anything like the degree to which these characterize Indian cooking. Gentler herbs and spices are most prevalent here.

Our dinner did not include Turkish coffee, largely because none of us likes it enough to warrant buying the special pot needed to make it. It would be inappropriate, however, for an inveterate coffee drinker not to bow at least in the direction of Turkey for its contribution in introducing coffee to the Western world. An Italian traveler to Turkey reported that the drink was served frequently both hot and cold and commented that, "It is also said that when drunk after supper, it prevents those who consume it from feeling sleepy. For that reason, students who wish to read into the late hours are fond of it." Sound familiar?

Since alcohol is prohibited by the religion of most Middle Eastern people, there are no indigenous wines or liquors other than those produced in Israel (and, of course, in Greece, which is technically part of the Middle East but which we have covered in another chapter). While we did use an Israeli white wine, you can, if it is hard to find in your area, substitute a more easily available white wine.

Whatever you drink, your appropriate toast might well be the Hebrew one, "l'chayim"—To Life!

SHOPPING SOURCES

The only items required by the menu which you might have trouble finding in your local supermarket are the burghul (sometimes listed as Bulgar Wheat), tahini and the Turkish coffee and coffee pot if you want them. Pine nuts, sometimes labeled pignolia, are now available in most areas but mail order sources for these too are indicated.

AMERICAN TEA, COFFEE AND SPICE CO., 1511 Champa Street, Denver, Colorado, 80202. Catalogue available. (Burghul, tahini, Turkish coffee and coffee pot, pine nuts.)

ANTONE'S, P. O. Box 3352, Houston, Texas 77001. Catalogue available. (Burghul, Turkish coffee and coffee pot, pine nuts.)

CHEESE VILLAGE LTD., 3 Greenwich Avenue, New York, N. Y. 10011. No catalogue available but will fill mail orders. (Burghul, tahini.)

PAPRIKAS WEISS, 1546 Second Avenue, New York, N. Y. 10028. Catalogue 25¢. (Burghul, pine nuts, Turkish coffee and coffee pot.)

H. ROTH AND SON, 1577 First Avenue, New York, N. Y. 10028 or 968 Second Avenue, New York, N. Y. 10022. Catalogue available. (Burghul, tahini, pine nuts, Turkish coffee and coffee pot.)

Middle East

FALAFEL

This deep fried mixture of chick peas and fine wheat is not only traditionally eaten as an hors d'oeuvre throughout the Middle East, but, placed in the hollow of a piece of Arab bread, is a popular snack sold by street vendors—a kind of Mid-East equivalent of the hot dog. We suggest you serve it just that way with your predinner drinks. Place a bowl of falafel and a platter of Arab bread on the cocktail table and let the guests make up their own sandwiches.

Just in case you feel guilty about using something as modern as an electric blender for this dish, remember that the old world is changing—a dry falafel "ready mix" is becoming very popular in the lands where everything used to be pounded by hand with mortar and pestle!

4 cups canned chick peas
1 cup fine burghul
3 cups coarsely crumbled white bread
½ cup lemon juice
1 tablespoon garlic, minced
½ teaspoon red pepper, crushed
1 teaspoon coriander, ground
1 teaspoon cumin, ground
2 teaspoons salt
¼ cup parsley, chopped
oil for deep frying

1. Drain chick peas and rinse under cold running water.
2. Place the burghul in a bowl and cover with water. Let it soak for 15 minutes and then drain it in a sieve. In another bowl, treat the crumbled white bread the same

202

way. Squeeze excess water out of both the bread and the burghul with your hands.

3. Place the chick peas, lemon juice, garlic, parsley and seasonings in an electric blender and blend at high speed for 1 minute. Transfer the mixture to a large mixing bowl.

4. Add the burghul and white bread to the mixing bowl and mix well. Form into firm balls about 1 and ½ inches in diameter and place the balls on wax paper. Let them stand at room temperature for an hour. They can then be refrigerated, if necessary, until you are ready to deep-fry them.

5. Heat 2 inches of oil in a deep fryer to 375° and fry the falafel balls for about 3 minutes until they turn golden. Remove to paper toweling with a slotted spoon as they are ready.

ARAB BREAD

2 packages dry yeast
2 cups lukewarm water
1 teaspoon sugar
8 cups flour
2 teaspoons salt
3 tablespoons oil

1. Place half of the water in a bowl and sprinkle the yeast and sugar over it. Cover and let stand in a warm place for 7-8 minutes until it is bubbly.

2. Sift the flour and salt into a mixing bowl. Make a well in the center and pour in the bubbling yeast mixture.

Mix, add the remaining cup of warm water, mix again, then add half the oil and mix again.

3. Turn the dough out on a lightly floured board and knead for 10 minutes until the dough is elastic and doesn't stick to your fingers.
4. Lightly oil the bottom and sides of a bowl and turn the ball of dough around so that all sides are lightly greased. Cover the bowl with a dampened tea towel and let stand in a warm place until the dough doubles in bulk. (This is a somewhat stiff dough and may take close to 2 hours unless your kitchen is very warm.)
5. Punch the dough down with your fist and knead it briefly again. On a lightly floured board, divide the dough into 12 pieces and roll each one into a circle no more than ¼ inch thick. Spread the rounds out on your board or on a lightly floured cloth. Cover with a cloth and let stand for another hour until the loaves rise again.
6. Set the oven at 500° and let it heat for 10 minutes. Sprinkle the remaining oil on baking sheets and brush it over the whole surface until the sheets are lightly oiled but there is no excess oil floating around. Put the baking sheets in the oven to heat for another 10 minutes.
7. Place the loaves on the baking sheets and bake for 8 minutes without opening the oven door.
8. Place the loaves immediately on a rack to cool. If the bread is not to be eaten immediately, cover it well and reheat briefly just before serving.

STUFFED BASS WITH TAHINI SAUCE

To make this dish you will want a bass that weighs

about 7 pounds when the head and tail have been removed and the fish has been cleaned and boned. Since bass tend to have heavy heads, you will need to start with a bass weighing about 12 pounds. If large bass are not available, you can, of course, use 2 smaller fish as long as you have about 7 pounds net. The fish should be split down one side and boned so that it is ready for stuffing.

> 7 *lb split bass (see note above)*
> 1 *and ½ lbs fillets of bass*
> 6 *tablespoons oil*
> 1 *and ⅓ cups onion, chopped*
> 1 *and ½ cups pine nuts*
> ¼ *cup butter*
> ¾ *cup raw rice*
> ¼ *cup parsley, chopped*
> 2 *tablespoons salt*

1. Cook the rice.
2. While the rice is cooking, melt the butter in a saucepan and cook the chopped onion and pine nuts over a gentle flame until the nuts are slightly brown.
3. Heat the oil in a skillet and cook the bass fillets until done (about 5 minutes). Flake the fillets into a large mixing bowl.
4. Add the cooked rice, the onion and nut mixture, the parsley and salt to the flaked fish and mix gently.
5. Pat the bass dry and sprinkle inside and out with salt. Spread the filling on one side of the inner surface of the bass and fold the other side over. Put heavy duty aluminum foil on a cookie sheet, leaving about 6 inches of foil on each side. Place the fish on the foil and crumple the excess foil around the edges of the fish, making a

good tight little wall on the open side to keep the stuffing in. Brush the top of the fish with oil.
6. Bake at 500° for 10 minutes, then reduce heat to 400° and bake for an additional 30-35 minutes until top of fish is nicely browned.

Tahini Sauce

> ¼ *cup parsley, chopped*
> 2 *cloves garlic*
> 1 *cup water*
> ¾ *cup lemon juice*
> ½ *teaspoon salt*
> 2 *cups tahini*

1. Put the garlic, parsley and a little of the water into an electric blender and blend for 10 seconds.
2. Add all remaining ingredients and blend for half a minute.
3. Pass sauce in a gravy boat.

(You will find an electric knife a great help in cutting the fish into neat serving portions.)

STEWED CARROTS

This dish is a good example of how the cooking of Israel has been affected by the influx of migrants from Europe— and vice versa. Elaborate carrot stews, frequently made with beef and potatoes or dumplings, are characteristic of central European Jewish cooking. In fact, the word for this kind of elaborate carrot dish, Tsimmes, has also come to mean a great—and usually unnecessary—fuss. So far as the dish is concerned, if you generally find cooked carrots bland and uninteresting, you will join me in feeling that this particular fuss is not superfluous.

Notwithstanding the fact that the concept may be European in origin, this recipe clearly shows the Middle-Eastern influence.

> *1 lb carrots, peeled and cubed*
> *1 cup water*
> *¾ cup orange juice*
> *¾ cup dry red wine*
> *½ cup golden raisins*
> *3 tablespoons butter*
> *1 cinnamon stick*
> *5 cloves*

1. Put the cloves in a square of cheesecloth and tie shut.
2. Put all ingredients, except the carrots, in a pot and simmer for 10 minutes.
3. Add carrots and simmer for 1 hour. Discard clove bag and the cinnamon stick.

CHEESE STUFFED PEPPERS

> 10 *medium green peppers*
> 1 *eggplant*
> 1 *lb cottage cheese*
> 2 *tablespoons flour*
> ¼ *cup parsley, chopped*
> 1 *egg*
> 3 *tablespoons butter*
> 2 *and* ½ *cups tomato sauce*
>   *salt and pepper*

1. Pare eggplant and cut it in ¼ inch rounds. Sprinkle the slices liberally with salt and place them in a glass or ceramic dish for ½ hour to drain. Dice.
2. Cut tops off the peppers and remove seeds. Wash and dice the tops.
3. Mix the diced eggplant, pepper tops, cheese, flour, parsley and egg together and stuff the peppers with the mixture, adding a little salt and pepper to taste.
4. Just before you're ready to bake the peppers, dot the top of each with butter, place them in a baking dish and pour the tomato sauce over and around the peppers.
5. Bake at 400° for 30 minutes. (Note that this is the same temperature needed to bake the fish so that you can have both dishes in the oven simultaneously.)

CHOCOLATE HAZELNUT CAKE
The Cake

> 6 *egg whites*
> 6 *tablespoons sugar*
> ½ *lb shelled hazelnuts*
> 2 *tablespoons matzoh meal (or fine bread crumbs)*

1. Grind the nuts coarsely in a blender or by placing them between two sheets of aluminum foil and crushing them with a rolling pin.
2. Beat egg whites until stiff.
3. Fold the sugar into the egg whites, then fold in the nuts and then the matzoh meal.
4. Pour the batter into 2 Teflon cake pans. (If your cake pans are not Teflon-lined, butter and lightly flour the pans.)
5. Bake at 350° for 30 minutes.

The Filling

> 6 *egg yolks*
> 11 *tablespoons sugar*
> 1 *cup milk*
> 5 *ounces cooking chocolate*
> 1 *tablespoon butter, softened to room temperature*
> ½ *cup whole shelled hazelnuts*

1. Melt the chocolate in the top of a double boiler.
2. Beat the egg yolks with 7 tablespoons of the sugar until the mixture is lemon-colored.
3. Add the egg yolk mixture to the melted chocolate in the double boiler. Stir, then add the butter and the milk. Cook mixture until thickened, stirring frequently. Allow the mixture to cool.
4. Spread the cooled chocolate mixture over the top of one layer of the cake, put the other cake layer on top and spread balance of frosting over the top.
5. Heat the remaining 4 tablespoons of sugar in a small pan until it turns liquid. Brown over a very low flame. Stir in hazelnuts to coat them with melted sugar.
6. Pour the coated hazelnuts onto a buttered plate to cool. Break the nut clump into small pieces and put the pieces in the frosting on top of the cake.

BRAZIL

Quentao

Cream of Cucumber Soup

Feijoada
(meats with black beans and rice)

Beer Twists

Coconut Cream Sponge Cake

Brazilian Demitasse

Obviously, a mere twenty Eat-Ins can't begin to cover all the countries of the world. Brazil was a little bit of a bonus because the strong African and Portuguese influences in Brazilian cuisine gave us a little taste of things to come when Portugal and some of the Central African countries show up on our culinary itinerary.

While native Indian and Portuguese elements are strong in Brazilian cooking, the single strongest influence is that of the Africans. In many ways, blacks brought from Africa as slave labor fared better in Brazil than in most other parts of the Western Hemisphere because the climate and country most resembled that which they had left behind. The Portuguese ladies left the cooking to the blacks who promptly proceeded to cook it the way **they** liked it. After all, if dende oil was substituted for olive oil in cooking what the mistress ordered, they could always justify it as dende oil was easily extracted from an African palm which flourished well in Brazil while olive trees did not.

The chief contribution of the Indians to today's cuisine is manioc, also known as cassava. This is a root which grows in two forms, sweet and bitter, and presents another example of man's courage in experimenting with food. The bitter manioc has a poisonous acid which the Indians learned to drain off so that only the edible portion of the root was left. One sometimes wonders how many cooks fell by the potside while the system of removing the poisonous acid was being developed!

While toasted manioc is usually served with the feijoada, we omitted it from our dinner. We felt that black beans and rice together were about all the starch our North American digestions could absorb in a single meal. Addi-

213

tionally, manioc is difficult to obtain locally even in large cities. You could substitute farina, briefly toasted in the oven before serving.

The feijoada is as much **the** national dish of Brazil as goulash is of Hungary. There are all kinds of variations, and several meats can be added to those we used. A lavish feijoada can keep the cook pretty busy for a 24-hour period. Ours, we hasten to say, won't. And please don't get cautious about serving rice and black beans together. The spicy bean mixture over the bland rice is a fantastic combination and, while you may not adopt the Brazilian conviction that no lunch is complete without beans and rice, you will make a new taste discovery if this is your first experience with this dish.

While we did have rolls, bread and rolls are really a comparatively new element in Brazilian cooking and not an enormously popular one. Beans and rice are the more traditional staples. If you find you're able to serve the toasted manioc, you might want to substitute it for the rolls. Don't, however, make any substitutions for Phyllis' cake. It would be a pleasure at any time but it's particularly apt as a cool ending to a well-spiced meal.

If you're feeling adventurous, you might try serving maté, an herb tea, or Brazilian demitasse with your dinner. The maté is brewed like any other tea so you won't find a recipe for it. You will find one for the Brazilian coffee. If you can't find Brazilian coffee locally and don't want to bother ordering by mail, you can substitute Italian espresso coffee which is widely available.

SHOPPING SOURCES

AMERICAN TEA, COFFEE AND SPICE CO., 1511 Champa St., Denver, Colorado, 80202. Catalogue available. (black beans, maté, Brazilian coffee)

ANTONE'S, P. O. Box 3352, Houston, Texas 77001. Catalogue available. (dried beef, chorizo, black beans, jalapenos hot peppers, maté)

CASA MONEO, 210 West 14th Street, New York, N. Y. 10011. Catalogue available. (dried beef, chorizo, black beans, jalapenos hot peppers)

Brazil

QUENTAO

For this dinner you can, if you prefer, use almost any rum cocktail of which you're fond and you'll be right in the proper Brazilian drinking spirit. Somewhere along the line, however, we seem to have developed a weakness for warmed drinks and this may explain why we chose this one. Quentao is usually served on St. John's Day, June 24, which you may remember is the cold season in Brazil. St. John is considered the sponsor of marriage and very popular with young girls looking for husbands. It may be a little unsporting to handicap young benedicts with Quentao on Sadie Hawkins Day but our experience indicates that it probably works.

> 2 *bottles domestic burgundy*
> 5 *quarts club soda*
> 16 *cloves*
> 8 *cinnamon sticks*
> 2 *and ½ sliced lemons*

1. Put all ingredients except the wine in a pot. Bring to a boil and let the mixture boil gently for ½ hour.
2. Reduce the heat, cover the pot and let the mixture simmer for 1 hour.
3. Strain. Add the wine, mix and serve hot.

CREAM OF CUCUMBER SOUP

> 3 large cucumbers
> 1 and ½ cups water
> 3 slices Bermuda onion
> ½ teaspoon salt
> ½ teaspoon white pepper
> 6 tablespoons flour
> 3 cups chicken stock
> 1 and ¼ cups heavy sweet cream or
>   yogurt*
> 2 tablespoons chives, minced

1. Peel, seed and slice the cucumbers.
2. Place cucumbers, water, onion, salt and pepper in a saucepan and cook, covered, over a medium flame until cucumbers are tender. This will take about 10 minutes if your cucumbers are sliced thin.
3. Pour mixture into a blender and blend until smooth.
4. Mix the flour with ¾ cup of the chicken stock in a saucepan. Add the remainder of the chicken stock gradually, stirring after each addition. Add the cucumber purée.
5. Cook over low heat for about 5 minutes, stirring. Refrigerate.
6. Just before serving, stir in the sweet cream or yogurt. Sprinkle chives over each portion.

*Yogurt is not really indigenous to Brazilian cooking. We've indicated it as a substitute if you think your group will settle for less authenticity and fewer calories.

Brazil

FEIJOADA

If you want to prepare this dish early in the day, go as far as Step 8, cover the meat and beans and let them stand at room temperature until half an hour before serving time. You can then proceed to Step 9.

> 3 cups black beans
>   small smoked tongue (uncooked)
> 1 small rack of spareribs
> 1 lb lean chuck
> ¾ lb Canadian bacon (unsliced)
> 1 lb chorizo (or hot Italian sausage)
> ¾ lb small fresh pork sausages
> ¾ lb dried beef
> 2 medium onions, chopped
> 3 cloves garlic, minced
> 1 cup canned, drained plum tomatoes
> 1 hot pepper (or 3 bottled or canned jalapenos peppers) seeded and minced
> 2 tablespoons oil
> 2 cups raw rice
>   peeled, sliced oranges

The Night Before

Soak the beans, tongue and dried beef overnight in 3 separate pans of cold water.

The Day of the Dinner

1. Place the tongue and the dried beef in a pot with enough cold water to cover them. Bring to a boil, reduce heat and simmer for 5 minutes. Drain and rinse the meat. Replace the meat in the pot and cover with fresh water. Bring to a boil, reduce heat and simmer for 1 hour.

2. When the tongue and dried beef have simmered for an hour, add the spareribs, Canadian bacon and chorizo or Italian sausage to the same pot. (Prick the sausage with a fork in several places before cooking it.) Simmer for 10 minutes more and remove all the meats from the pot.

3. While the meats are cooking, drain the soaking water off the beans and place the beans in the largest pot available. Cover with water about 1 and ½ inches higher than the beans. Bring to a boil, reduce heat and simmer, covered, for 1 hour.

4. When the tongue has cooled enough for handling, remove the skin and the bone and gristle from the end.

5. When the beans have simmered for 1 hour, put all of the meat except the chuck into the bean pot. Cover and cook 1 and ½ hours. Then add the chuck and cook 1 hour more or until the beans and meat are all tender. Remove the pot from the stove.

6. Remove the meats from the pot. Cut the spareribs into individual ribs and slice all the other meats except the small pork sausages. Set the meats aside.

7. Skim any fat from the top of the beans. Remove 2 cups of beans and 2 cups of bean liquid.

8. Melt the oil in a large skillet and cook the onion and garlic until the onion is transparent but not brown.

Add the tomatoes and pepper and cook gently for 5 minutes, stirring. Add the 2 cups of beans and mash with the back of a wooden spoon. Add the bean liquid gradually. Simmer 15 minutes, stirring frequently.

9. Half an hour before serving, heat the oven to 250° and place the meat in the oven to reheat. At the same time, drain the beans, reserving some of the liquid. Add the skillet mixture to the beans and stir. Simmer the bean mixture for 20 minutes.

10. At the same time you start Step 9, cook the 2 cups of raw rice by your usual method.

11. To serve, it is traditional to place the sliced tongue down the center of the platter and to place the smoked meats on one side and the fresh meats on the other. A little of the reserved bean liquid may be poured over the meats. The beans are served in a separate bowl and, as they help themselves, the guests usually put the beans over the rice and eat the two vegetables together. The sliced oranges can be used to garnish the meat platter or can be served separately. They serve as a pleasant fresh contrast to the spicy meats and beans.

BEER TWISTS

2 cups flour
½ lb sweet butter (unsoftened)
1 tablespoon sugar
¾ cup beer

The Night Before

1. Cut butter into flour with a pastry blender. Add sugar and beer and mix well.
2. Turn the dough out on a lightly floured board and knead until it is no longer sticky. Cover the dough and refrigerate it overnight.

To Bake the Rolls

1. Tear off chunks of dough the size of a large walnut. Roll each piece between your palms into a 2 inch cylinder. Twist each cylinder 2 or 3 times and place on an ungreased cookie sheet.
2. Bake at 400° for 20 minutes.

   Note: These can be sprinkled with powdered sugar while they are still warm from the oven, but this makes them a little too sweet for our taste as a dinner roll.

COCONUT CREAM SPONGE CAKE

> 5 *eggs, separated*
> ½ *cup sugar*
> 1 *and* ⅓ *cups muscatel*
> 1 *and* ¼ *cups flour*
> 1 *tablespoon butter*
> ¼ *teaspoon cinnamon*

Brazil

1. Place the egg whites in large bowl of electric mixer. Beat until whites form soft peaks, then start adding sugar gradually. Continue beating until whites are stiff and glossy.
2. In a separate bowl, beat the yolks and ⅓ cup wine with a fork or wire whisk.
3. Pour the yolk mixture over the egg whites and fold into the whites with a rubber spatula. Add the flour gradually, folding it into the mixture with the spatula.
4. Preheat oven to 350°. Rub the tablespoon of butter over the bottom and sides of a large cake pan or an 8 x 12 baking dish. Pour the cake mixture into the pan and smooth the top with the spatula.
5. Bake cake for 30 minutes. As soon as you remove it from the oven, turn it out on a cake rack to cool.
6. Put the cool cake on a serving dish. Mix the cinnamon with the remaining cup of muscatel and sprinkle the wine mixture over the top of the cake. Let the cake absorb the wine while you prepare the coconut cream topping.

Coconut Cream Topping

> ¼ *lb shredded coconut*
> 2 *and ½ cups hot water (not boiling)*
> 1 *cup sugar*
> 5 *egg yolks*

1. Put the coconut and the hot water in a blender and blend at medium speed for half a minute.
2. Place a fine strainer over a bowl and pour the coconut mixture through the strainer, pressing down with the

back of a wooden spoon to get all the milk out. Discard the solids.

3. Reserve ¾ cup of the coconut milk. Put the rest in a saucepan with the sugar and cook over medium heat, stirring, until the syrup reaches 230° on a candy thermometer. (If you have no thermometer, keep a cup of ice water near the stove and drop a bit of syrup in the water to test it; it will have cooked enough when the syrup dropped into the ice water immediately hardens.) Remove the pan from the heat.

4. In the mixing bowl of an electric beater, beat the egg yolks until they are lemon-colored. Add the remaining ¾ cup of coconut milk and then 2 tablespoons of the hot syrup, beating after each addition.

5. Pour the egg yolk mixture gradually into the pan of syrup. Cook over very low heat, stirring constantly for 15 minutes. Do not let the sauce come to a boil.

6. Pour the coconut cream mixture over the cake. You can, if you like, sprinkle some additional grated coconut over the top.

7. Refrigerate the cake for at least 2 hours before serving. If you're transporting the cake to the dinner, pop it into the refrigerator the minute you arrive so that it will be well chilled at serving time.

BRAZILIAN DEMITASSE

¾ cup ground coffee
7 and ½ cups water

Brazil

1. Heat the water to just below the boiling point.
2. Stir in the coffee, remove the pan from the stove and let it stand for 1 minute. Restir.
3. Line a strainer with a piece of flannel and pour the coffee through the lined strainer directly into the pot from which the coffee will be served. (Most people will want sugar but cream is not ordinarily served with this type of coffee.)

IRELAND

MENU

Potato Soup

Dublin Beer Batter Prawns

Fried Parsley Garnish

Creamed Carrots

Cabbage Salad

Soda Bread

Apple Tart with Custard Sauce

Irish Coffee

GUINNESS STOUT

We originally chose Ireland because Pat thought this would be a fine excuse for wheedling the recipe for Dublin Beer Batter Prawns out of her favorite Irish restauranteur. As you can see, she succeeded. The rest of us had a little more of a problem in picking our courses, since most of the people who talk or write about Irish cooking seem to lean heavily on nostalgia as the principal ingredient. And that's very hard to reproduce in an American kitchen where you'd have a little trouble baking bread over a turf fire or carrying your fish home from the harbor in a bucket of seawater "alive alive-O." We did succeed in turning out a fine dinner and one which we heartily recommend for a winter evening.

Irish cooking is well designed for the often cold climate. Much of the objective is to warm your insides so your outside won't feel the chill quite so much—an objective shared by the ubiquitous hot morning porridge and the equally ubiquitous Irish whiskey. Hot soup is a mainstay and there are those who maintain that the best soups of all are those made by throwing last night's leftovers into the pot. Our potato soup is less adventurous than that but very good notwithstanding.

It's a little startling to those of us who remember the great Irish potato famine of the nineteenth century to realize that the potato was not at all indigenous to Ireland. It was introduced from America in the seventeenth century. It thrived so well in the damp Irish soil and such large quantities could be grown on a small plot of ground that it became the indispensable staple, and the failure of the crop in 1845 was enough to plunge the country into dire straits and to start the wave of Irish emigration to the United States. Two interesting but (I think!) unrelated facts about the potato. Fact number 1: it was at one time considered an aphrodisiac. Fact number 2: some experts have blamed the beginning of the population explosion on the cultivation of the potato—not because of its allegedly aphrodisiac qualities but because it enabled people with even a small amount of land to provide large families with basic food.

Ireland raises excellent beef and lamb but, as you can see, we stayed away from the traditional Irish stew and corned beef and cabbage which have in effect been absorbed into American cooking. Ireland also enjoys excellent fish, including superb salmon, lobster (much of which is exported to Europe's luxury restaurants) and prawns. We'll have a brief semantic stop here: as you may have discovered the hard way in your European travels, large shrimp are known in the British Isles as prawns. Just to confuse the issue a little further, the famous Dublin Bay prawns are not shrimp at all but a species of lobster. If you're now thoroughly confused, take a deep breath, ask your fish man for the largest shrimp he can find for you and plunge into the relative simplicity of the kitchen again.

Elizabeth claims she got the best assignment of this dinner—the bread and wine. Irish breads are quick and easy to make because they are, by and large, not yeast breads. They use baking powder rather than yeast as the leavening. There is no rising period and the time from start to oven is so brief that you almost begin to understand why an Irish woman can casually knock off a couple of breads in an afternoon for what is called "six o'clock tea" but which is really light supper.

I think Elizabeth's real enjoyment of her task lay in the fact that she and Irwin dutifully tried out recipes for Irish coffee for many nights before she declared herself satisfied with the results. I'm not sure whether they were even trying

different recipes toward the end, but she says it sure is an improvement over testing vegetable recipes.

It would be inappropriate for you to have to wait for the end of dinner for any alcoholic refreshment. You can have the Guinness Stout with your dinner and if even that is too long to wait, you can try a Black Velvet before dinner—pour some champagne into a glass, add twice as much stout and drink up!

Ireland

POTATO SOUP

If the soup is to be transported to dinner, stop after Step 5 and add the cream and reheat the soup just before serving.

7 medium potatoes (3 lbs)
3 medium onions
3 tablespoons butter
4 cups milk
6 cups chicken stock
1 tablespoon salt
¼ teaspoon white pepper
1 cup light sweet cream
5 strips bacon
¼ cup snipped chives

1. Peel and slice the onions and potatoes.
2. Melt the butter in a large saucepan. Add the sliced onions and cook over a very low flame until tender but not brown.
3. Add the potatoes, chicken stock, milk, salt and pepper. Cover the pan and cook over a very low flame for 1 hour.
4. Cut the bacon in small pieces and sauté until crisp. Remove from pan with a slotted spoon and set bacon bits aside.
5. When the soup has cooked for an hour, put it through the blender at high speed. Return to saucepan.
6. Add cream and cook slowly until the soup is just hot but not at the boiling point.
7. Garnish with bacon bits and chives sprinkled on each serving.

DUBLIN BEER BATTER PRAWNS

As long as you're going to be deep-frying anyway, you might consider tossing in some fried parsley, which is delicious and decorative but for which you'd hesitate to cook up a fresh pot of oil. Wash a quantity of parsley sprigs with a bit of stem still attached and dry thoroughly. (If they're at all wet, they'll make a most unpleasant splash when you put them in the hot oil.) Just before you start frying the shrimp, put the parsley in a wire basket and lower it into the oil just for a moment until it stops sputtering. Remove the basket and proceed with the shrimp.

40–50 of the largest shrimp you can find; you'll have to judge by the size how many per serving you'll need. The bigger the better.

3 cups cake flour
4 eggs, beaten
1 and ½ tablespoons salt
6 tablespoons melted butter
2 and ¼ cups Guinness or Watney ale oil for deep-frying

The Night Before

1. Measure out the ale and let it stand for an hour until it goes flat.
2. Mix the flour, eggs, salt and butter together. Then add the ale and mix again.
3. Cover batter and refrigerate overnight.

Ireland

The Day of the Dinner

1. Shell and devein shrimp but leave the tail shell on. Rinse shrimp and pat thoroughly dry.
2. Heat oil to 350°. Dip each shrimp in the batter, holding it by the tail shell.
3. Deep-fry the shrimp a few at a time. Put the finished ones on a baking sheet lined with paper towel in a very low oven to stay warm while the rest are being cooked.
4. Serve the sauce on the side, preferably in small individual glass cups such as you use for serving melted butter with lobster.

The Sauce

1 and ½ tablespoons cornstarch
¾ cup beer
1 and ½ tablespoons soy sauce
1 and ¼ cups pineapple juice
6 tablespoons cider vinegar
6 tablespoons brown sugar
4 and ½ tablespoons Worcestershire sauce
¾ teaspoon salt
¾ teaspoon pepper
6 tablespoons raisins
½ teaspoon whole cloves, tied in a cheese-cloth bag
3 tablespoons butter

1. Mix the cornstarch and beer together in a saucepan, stirring until smooth.

2. Add all remaining ingredients except the butter.
3. Heat the mixture over a low flame for 20 minutes. Add butter and continue cooking until butter is melted.
4. Remove and discard the cheesecloth bag of cloves.

   Note: The sauce can be made early in the day and reheated just before serving.

CREAMED CARROTS

24 *young carrots*
 6 *tablespoons butter*
 1 *cup milk*
   salt and pepper
 1 *cup heavy cream*
 4 *egg yolks*
 2 *tablespoons parsley, finely chopped*

1. Trim and peel carrots. Cut each one lengthwise and then cut each half in two.
2. Melt butter over moderate heat and add milk, pepper and salt. Add carrots and cook gently for about 30 minutes or until tender.
3. Remove the pan from the stove and remove the carrots with a slotted spoon.
4. Combine the egg yolks and cream in a small bowl and beat with a fork. Add to the egg mixture 4 or 5 tablespoons of the hot liquid from the pot and stir well.
5. Add the egg mixture to the pot and reheat over a very low flame, stirring with a whisk, until the mixture is thickened. Don't let it boil!

Ireland

6. Correct seasoning if necessary. Replace carrots in pot and add parsley.

Note: If the carrots are to be transported to the dinner, stop before reheating the sauce (Step 5) and carry the sauce and the carrots to the dinner in separate containers. Then proceed from where you left off, just being sure to let the carrots simmer for a minute in the finished sauce to reheat them.

CABBAGE SALAD

2 lbs white cabbage
1 tablespoon parsley, minced
1 tablespoon chives, minced
¾ cup olive oil
¼ cup lemon juice
1 teaspoon salt
⅛ teaspoon white pepper
2 cloves garlic, split

1. Two hours before serving, mix the olive oil, lemon juice, salt, and pepper together. Add the cut cloves of garlic.
2. Cut cabbage in quarters and remove the hard core. Cut each quarter in the thinnest possible slices.
3. Soak cabbage in cold water for half an hour. Drain and roll it up in a Turkish towel to remove all moisture.
4. To serve, remove the garlic from the dressing, restir the dressing and toss with cabbage, parsley and chives.

IRISH SODA BREAD

> 5 *cups whole wheat flour*
> 2 *and ½ cups white flour*
> ⅓ *cup sugar*
> 2 *teaspoons baking soda*
> 1 *teaspoon salt*
> ½ *lb sweet butter*
> 2 *eggs*
> 2 *and ¼ cups buttermilk*

1. Mix the two flours, sugar, baking soda and salt together in a large bowl.
2. Cut the butter in with a pastry blender.
3. In another bowl, beat the eggs lightly and add the buttermilk. Mix.
4. Make a well in the center of the flour mixture and add the egg mixture gradually, mixing with a wooden spoon after each addition.
5. Turn the dough out onto a lightly floured board and knead until smooth.
6. Divide the dough into 2 halves and shape each half into a round ball. Flatten the tops slightly with the palm of your hand and, with a sharp knife make an x cut, half an inch deep on the top of each loaf.
7. Place the loaves on a lightly buttered or Teflon baking sheet. Bake at 400° for 50 minutes.

Ireland

APPLE TART WITH CUSTARD SAUCE

Baking a pie on a flat plate instead of your usual pie pan may seem odd, but do resist the temptation to adapt the recipe to your normal pie baking method. This is a lovely buttery tart and it wouldn't be quite the same if made in the standard American shape.

3 cups unsifted flour
⅛ teaspoon salt
¾ lb cold sweet butter
5 tablespoons ice water
5 large cooking apples
3 tablespoons sugar
1 teaspoon nutmeg

1. Add the salt to the flour. Work in the butter with a pastry blender.
2. Add the ice water and work into a stiff dough. Refrigerate for 1 hour.
3. Turn the pastry onto a lightly floured board. Cut off ⅓ of it and roll it into a circle large enough to cover a 10-inch ovenproof china or aluminum plate. Cover the plate with the pastry circle, pressing it down gently.
4. Peel, core and slice the apples. Place them on the crust, leaving about half an inch around the edge of the crust uncovered. Sprinkle the sugar and nutmeg over the apples.
5. Roll the remaining pastry into a circle about an inch larger all around than the plate.
6. Brush the empty edges of the bottom crust with water

236

and place the top crust over the filling, pressing the top edge down on the moistened edge of the bottom crust.

7. Trim the edges neatly and make two small gashes in the center of the top crust.
8. Bake at 425° for 15 minutes, then reduce the heat to 325° for 45 minutes or until the crust is golden brown.

Custard Sauce

1 and ½ cups milk
2 teaspoons cornstarch
1 tablespoon sugar
1 egg yolk
½ teaspoon vanilla

1. In a heavy saucepan (off the stove) combine ¼ cup of the milk and the cornstarch. Stir with a whisk until the cornstarch is dissolved.
2. Add the rest of the milk and the sugar. Cook over moderate heat, stirring, until the sauce thickens and comes to a boil.
3. Break up the egg yolk with a fork in a small bowl. Stir in 2 or 3 tablespoons of the sauce. Return this mixture to the saucepan and bring the mixture to a boil again, stirring constantly.
4. Remove the pan from the heat and stir in the vanilla.
5. You have a choice of serving the pie and custard sauce warm or cold or one of each. For serving convenience for this kind of dinner, you might serve the pie at room temperature and the custard warmed slightly.

Ireland

IRISH COFFEE

> *15 oz Irish whiskey*
> *65 oz hot strong black coffee*
> *8 teaspoons sugar*
> *whipped cream*

1. Mix whiskey, coffee and sugar together.
2. Divide the coffee mixture into 10 Irish Coffee glasses or cups.
3. Top each serving with whipped cream. Do not mix the cream into the coffee; let it float on top.

Note: If you need extra portions (or if you want to make smaller quantities) the proportions for each serving are 1½ ounces whiskey, 6½ ounces coffee and a scant teaspoon of sugar.

INDONESIA

MENU

Stir-fried Shrimp

Lamb Saté

Peanut Sauce

Fried Onion Flakes

Cucumber Pickles

Sweet and Spicy Salad

Orange Rice

Banana Fritters

Avocado Whip

HEINEKEN'S BEER

While there are common elements in the cuisine of the string of islands that comprise Indonesia, there is a range of variation from the somewhat ascetic cooking of the Muslims to the proverbially hedonistic feasting of such legendary islands as Bali. As late as the nineteenth century there was some cannibalism in islands such as Java but by the end of the century it had about disappeared—perhaps as a result of social development and perhaps because of the increasing complaint that human flesh (or "long pig") had lost its savor. To gourmets of the era, vegetarians made better eating than meat eaters and smoking ruined the flavor of a man altogether. Now, there's an antismoking argument the Surgeon General hasn't used yet!

Indonesian cooking reflects a number of influences. The Chinese were trading and in many cases immigrating to Indonesia before the birth of Christ. Centuries of Indian and Arab contact and many years of Dutch rule have also left their mark. Two of the most important pieces of cooking equipment are the grinding stone used for mixing spices (as in India) and the Chinese wok. Perhaps the single most important contribution of the Dutch to the cuisine was the introduction of beer. In the long run the Indonesians may have contributed more to Dutch cooking. Saté (barbecued chunks of marinated meat) and nasi goreng (fried rice) have become favorite snack as well as mealtime foods in Holland. And the Dutch acquired a passion for Rijsttafel resulting in its being included in any cookbook dealing with the cuisine of Holland.

Rijsttafel literally means a "rice table." The core of the meal is rice with multitudinous dishes of meats, poultry, fish, vegetables, salad, pickles, preserves and fruits served

241

as an accompaniment. An ordinary family meal might consist of five or six dishes—rice, one meat dish, one chicken or fish dish and two dishes of vegetables or pickled food. For an elegant dinner, however, there might be twenty or more dishes brought to the table by a line of serving men. Each dish was brought separately and a dinner was, therefore, characterized as a "ten boy dinner" or a "twenty boy dinner." Since the honor paid to the guest was considered in direct proportion to the number of dishes, the era of Dutch rule tended to stretch the banquet dishes considerably.

Meat is normally eaten in small quantities, not so much for economic reasons as for gustatory ones. Since variety of the foods in a meal is the essential element, a large steak or a slab of roast beef which would limit the diner's ability to enjoy a variety of tastes is generally considered unappetizing. Meat cut in small pieces with just a few pieces served to each diner along with a quantity of other dishes is much more typical. Dessert normally consists of fruit. Other desserts enjoy their greatest popularity during Ramadhan, the month in which people fast from sunrise to sunset. The 13 or 14-hour fast is traditionally broken by a sweet and, since schools are closed and this is a great time for family visiting, dessert-making as well as other cooking reaches its peak of activity during this period.

Bread is not indigenous to Indonesian cooking. A shrimp crisp called krupuk is made from tapioca and dried shrimp. It is usually bought already processed and is deep fried before serving. Since krupuk are not easily available here, you can substitute the somewhat smaller Chinese shrimp crisps which are more easily available. These too are deep fried.

Indonesia produces no wine of any interest. The Dutch beer which Indonesians adopted is eminently suitable. If, however, you want a wine with dinner, any good chilled dry white wine will do.

Indonesian food is not served in separate courses. All dishes are placed on the table or served simultaneously so that a variety of tastes can be experienced. For this menu, we suggest that you follow the custom and put everything on the table at one time. If your serving boys happen to have the night off, try a buffet arrangement with a judicious use of hot trays for the meat and rice.

Good eating!

SHOPPING SOURCES

AMERICAN TEA, COFFEE AND SPICE CO., 1511 Champa Street, Denver, Colorado 80202. Catalogue available. (tamarind extract)

MRS. De WILDT, 245-A Fox Gap Road, Bangor R. D. 3, Pennsylvania 18013. Catalogue available. (krupuk, unsweetened ground coconut, bamboo skewers; also carries a selection of Dutch, Japanese, Chinese and Indian specialties)

LES ECHALOTTES, Ramsey, New Jersey 07446. Catalogue 25¢. (krupuk)

H. ROTH AND SON, 1577 First Avenue, New York, N. Y. 10028 or 968 Second Avenue, New York, N. Y. 10022. Catalogue available. (tamarind)

TRINACRIA, 415 Third Avenue, New York, N. Y. 10016. Catalogue available. (tamarind, fresh chilies)

Note: Shrimp chips are available from any of the Chinese supply sources listed on p. 152.

Indonesia

STIR-FRIED SHRIMP

1 and ½ lbs raw shrimp
5 tablespoons vinegar
2 and ½ teaspoons salt
1 tablespoon sugar
1 teaspoon coriander
2 cloves garlic, minced
⅛ teaspoon ginger, ground
peanut oil for frying

1. Shell and devein shrimp, making a fairly deep cut along the back so that the shrimp are partially split.
2. Mix all other ingredients except the peanut oil and marinate the shrimp in the mixture for 2 hours.
3. Heat a quarter inch of oil in a skillet or electric frying pan and fry the shrimp, stirring frequently, for about 4 minutes.

LAMB SATÉ

4 lbs leg of lamb cut into ½ inch cubes
1 teaspoon salt
4 cloves garlic, minced
1 onion, grated
2 tablespoons brown sugar
3 tablespoons lemon juice
1 teaspoon tamarind juice*
¼ cup soy sauce
1 lime

244

1. Combine all the ingredients except the lamb and the lime and marinate the meat in the mixture for several hours.
2. Place several cubes of meat on bamboo skewers and broil or, better still, grill over a charcoal fire.
3. Squeeze a bit of lime juice over the meat before serving. The saté is served garnished with fried onion flakes and with the peanut sauce as a side dish.

*While bottled tamarind juice can be bought, you can also make the juice yourself by soaking a small piece of tamarind in ½ cup of warm water for half an hour. When the fruit is soft, squeeze out the liquid and discard the pulp.

PEANUT SAUCE

> ¼ lb coconut, shredded
> 2 and ½ cups hot water
> 8 oz crunchy peanut butter
> 2 tablespoons brown sugar
> 1 tablespoon hot chili, ground
> 2–inch piece of lemon rind
> ½ teaspoon salt
> ¼ teaspoon pepper

1. Put half of the coconut and half the hot water in a blender and blend at medium speed for 30 seconds. Pour the mixture into a strainer set over a bowl. Repeat the same procedure with the rest of the coconut and hot water.
2. With a wooden spoon, press down on the coconut in

the strainer to extract as much juice as possible. You should have 2 cups of thick coconut milk.
3. Place the coconut milk and all other ingredients in a saucepan and bring slowly to a boil, stirring frequently. Remove the sauce the moment it begins to boil.

FRIED ONION FLAKES

The onion flakes do not need to be served warm. They can, therefore, be made in advance and stored in a covered jar until dinnertime.

4 onions
peanut oil

1. Slice each onion in half lengthwise. Then, with the cut half of the onion down, slice each half in thin slices.
2. Heat enough peanut oil to cover the onions. Fry the onions carefully, stirring continuously until they are well-browned but not burned.
3. Pour the contents of the pan through a strainer immediately so that the oil is discarded. Break the onion slices into flakes with a fork.

CUCUMBER PICKLES

> 3 *chilies (red, green or mixed)*
> 5 *cucumbers*
> 2 *tablespoons salt*
> 1 *quart white vinegar*
> ½ *cup sugar*

1. Slice the chilies into thin rings. Rinse thoroughly under running cold water, removing seeds. (Be sure to wash your hands after you handle chilies, since the oils can be irritating to the skin.)
2. Wash the cucumbers but do not peel them. Cut each cucumber lengthwise in four pieces. With the tip of a teaspoon remove the seeds and pulp from the center of each quarter.
3. Cut the cucumbers into cubes. Sprinkle the salt over them and refrigerate for 1 hour. Rinse in cold water.
4. Bring the vinegar and sugar to a boil and cook until the sugar is dissolved.
5. Add the cucumber cubes and chili rings and bring the mixture to a boil again. Remove from the stove and let cool.
6. The pickles can be made well in advance and stored for a week or two.

Indonesia

SWEET AND SPICY SALAD

2 cups brown sugar
3 cups water
3 tablespoons peanut butter
5 teaspoons vinegar
1 teaspoon salt
1 and ½ teaspoons red pepper, crushed
1 and ½ cups carrots, shredded
1 and ½ cups cucumber, shredded
1 and ½ cups apples, diced
1 and ½ cups pears, diced

1. Combine the sugar and water in a saucepan. Bring to a boil, reduce heat and simmer for 10 minutes, stirring frequently.
2. Add the peanut butter and stir to dissolve. Remove the pan from the stove and add the vinegar, salt and crushed red pepper.
3. While the mixture is cooling, shred and dice the vegetables and fruits into a bowl.
4. Pour the cool mixture over the vegetables and fruits and refrigerate for at least 2 hours.
5. To serve, drain and discard the marinade.

ORANGE RICE

2 cups orange juice
3 cups water
rinds of 2 oranges
2 cups long-grained rice
¾ lb baby shrimp
1 medium onion, diced

1. Grate the orange rinds or pulverize them in an electric blender.
2. Place orange juice and water in a saucepan and bring to a boil. Add the ground rinds and the rice, reduce heat and simmer, covered, for 25 minutes.
3. While the rice is cooking, sauté the diced onion and the shrimp in a separate pan.
4. Mix the onion and shrimp into the rice before serving.

BANANA FRITTERS

1 cup sifted flour
pinch of salt
5 oz lukewarm water
5 bananas
1 egg white, beaten stiff
oil for deep frying
confectioners' sugar

1. Sift flour and salt into a bowl. Make a well in the middle and add the warm water a little at a time, stirring with a wooden spoon until batter is smooth.
2. Fold in the beaten egg white.
3. Peel the bananas and cut each in half crosswise. Make 2 or 3 parallel cuts down the length of each half but leave the end uncut. Gently spread the banana half into a fan shape.
4. Dip banana fans in batter and deep-fry until golden. Drain on absorbent paper.
5. Sprinkle bananas lightly with confectioners' sugar before serving.

Indonesia

AVOCADO WHIP

> 2 avocados
> juice of 2 lemons
> ¼ cup sugar
> 1 pint vanilla ice cream

1. Cut avocados in half and remove pits. Peel.
2. Put the avocado flesh in the blender and blend for 30 seconds. Then put the flesh through a sieve, forcing the fruit through with the back of a wooden spoon into a mixing bowl.
3. Add lemon juice and sugar to the fruit.
4. Add the ice cream and beat with a mixer until smooth.
5. Place the mixture in the freezer to chill but do not let it freeze. Serve in small sherbet glasses.

SPAIN

M E N U

Cocktails

Toasted Almonds

Quarter-of-an-Hour Soup

Spanish Garlic Steak

Catalan Salad

Vegetable Casserole

Sweet Bread

Natilla

QUITAPENAS MALAGA DULCE
HIJOS DE JOSE SUAREZ VILLALBA
BANDA AZUL 1967

While Spain has its share of great restaurants, the heart of the cuisine is in the home—partly for economic reasons and partly because of the fantastic (in today's world) tightness of the family structure. The long lunch period is still observed in Spain, not for gastronomic or health reasons but because the Spaniards still by and large consider it barbarous for a family not to eat together. The three hour lunch break is hardly conducive to easy living when office or shop workers sometimes have to travel an hour each way to get home for lunch and back to work. Except for highly paid executives who could afford to eat in restaurants near their offices, most people do not have the equivalent of the sandwich or hamburger shop (or, needless to say, the company cafeteria) available to American workers. Bringing one's sandwich to the office is not only considered undignified but anyone who didn't go home for lunch would be somewhat suspect to being not quite respectable.

Inconvenient as the custom may be, perhaps this is at least a partial explanation of why there appears to be less generation gap in Spain than one is aware of in other parts of the world. While the Spanish family is a patriarchal rather than a democratic unit, the generations do communicate and the family lunch is an important time for the exchange of the trivial news of the day which perhaps keeps the lines of communication open better than when they are reserved for major crises.

While I have no ambition to start a home-for-lunch movement or to emulate the Spanish family structure in other ways, I am a little wistfully envious of the Basque eating clubs. Each club consists of anywhere from forty to two-hundred members, all of whom contribute to the cooking. There are no social lines. The same club will have fishermen and lawyers on its roster; the only discrimination—alas!—is that the clubs are reserved for men only. Oh well, so is the New York Athletic Club and the Basque eating club sounds like more fun.

It is believed that olive trees were introduced by the Phoenicians as early as eighteen centuries before the birth of Christ and it would be hard to visualize Spain or Spanish cooking without olives and olive oil. Olives are used extensively in salads and in meat and vegetable dishes—a happy custom which has only recently begun to take hold in the United States in those states most subject to Mexican cooking influence.

While Spanish traders and explorers played an enormous part in the spice trade, not enough of it appears to have stayed in Spain to influence the cooking heavily. Unlike Mexican food, with which it is sometimes confused by the novice, Spanish cooking is not heavily spiced. While the Spaniards were not particularly innovative with spices, they were the first inventors of tomato sauce at a time when the rest of Europe viewed with great suspicion any use of the tomato other than as an ornamental garden plant.

The wine, Banda Azul, 1967 is a red wine reputed to have been a favorite of Ernest Hemingway. I can't vouch for the literary association but the wine is good.

This dinner is a particularly easy one because it requires no ingredients that you are not likely to find in your local supermarket. Spanish olive oil and Spanish olives are excellent and should be used if available, but you don't really have to resort to mail order sources if you can get other oil and olives of first quality in your neighborhood store.

Spain

TOASTED ALMONDS

These are a little bit of a chore to prepare in comparison to the ease of opening a can of nuts. But they bear no resemblance to the canned kind and they can be made at your convenience a week or two ahead of time and stored in a tightly covered jar. Chore or not, if you have any vanity as a hostess, the chances are you'll add them to your permanent cocktail hour repertoire.

> *1 lb almonds*
> *¼ cup olive oil*
> *salt*

1. Shell the almonds.
2. Boil a pot of water. Take it off the stove and drop the almonds into the water for 30 seconds. Remove one almond with a spoon, run cold water over it and remove the brown skin. If the skin slips off easily, the almonds are ready. If not, let them stay in the water for a few seconds more.
3. Drain almonds and run cold water over them. Slip off the brown skins and place the almonds on paper towels to dry.
4. Heat oven to 325°. Dry almonds with paper towels and spread on a cookie sheet. Bake for 35 minutes, turning occasionally with a spatula.
5. Pour the olive oil into a bowl. While the almonds are still warm, dip them into the oil and remove promptly with a slotted spoon.
6. Sprinkle almonds liberally with salt and allow to air dry before placing in a covered container for storage.

QUARTER-OF-AN-HOUR SOUP

> *1 dozen littleneck clams*
> *1 lb shrimp*
> *4 oz slice of boiled ham, cubed*
> *2 medium onions, chopped*
> *3 tomatoes*
> *¼ cup raw rice*
> *3 slices white bread*
> *½ cup peas*
> *1 tablespoon paprika*
> *1 tablespoon salt*
> *⅛ teaspoon pepper*
> *5 tablespoons olive oil*
> *7 cups boiling water*
> *3 hard-boiled eggs*

1. Scrub clams with hard brush and set them in a pan of cold water for an hour to remove any sand. Then scrub them again.
2. Place clams in a pan with just enough water to cover and cook them until the shells begin to open. Remove each clam as it opens and set aside.
3. Line a strainer with a napkin and pour the clam broth through the napkin to remove any stray sand. Set 2 cups of the strained broth aside to use for the soup and use what is left over to parboil the rice.
4. Boil the leftover clam broth (plus a little more water if necessary) and drop the rice in for 3 minutes. Drain and set the rice aside.
5. In 2 tablespoons of the olive oil, lightly sauté the white bread (crusts removed) and then put the bread briefly through the blender at low speed or cut or tear it in small pieces.

6. Remove the skins from the tomatoes by dropping them in boiling water for a minute before peeling. Remove the seeds and either run the tomatoes briefly through the blender at low speed or chop them.
7. In the remaining 3 tablespoons of olive oil, sauté the ham cubes gently for 3-4 minutes. Add the chopped onion and cook until the onion is golden. Add the tomatoes and simmer for 5 more minutes.
8. Add the shelled and cleaned shrimp, boiling water, bread, paprika, salt, pepper, rice and peas. Cook for 15 minutes. Add the 2 cups of reserved clam broth and the clams.
9. Grate the hard-boiled eggs by putting them through a potato ricer or mashing with a potato masher.
10. If the soup is to be served immediately, add the grated eggs and let the soup simmer for 1 minute more. If the soup will be carried to the Eat-In, take the grated eggs separately and add them to the soup when you reheat it.

SPANISH GARLIC STEAK

10 *shell steaks, 1 inch thick*
10 *cloves garlic, minced*
½ *cup sherry*
½ *cup wine vinegar*
1 *cup olive oil*
¼ *cup green olives, chopped*
¼ *cup black olives, chopped*
salt

The Night Before

1. Combine all ingredients except the steak and salt. Mix the marinade well.
2. Pour the marinade over the steaks and refrigerate overnight. The steaks should be turned from time to time.

To Serve

1. Remove the steaks from the marinade and sprinkle meat with salt.
2. Broil the steaks. While they are broiling, heat the marinade.
3. Pour some of the marinade over each steak before serving.

CATALAN SALAD

Prepare a green salad with endive, lettuce and any other greens you fancy and garnish with sliced radishes and small pitted Spanish olives, green and red pepper rings and a few flat anchovies. This should be a decoratively arranged salad and should be mixed with the Xato Sauce at the table after all the guests have had an opportunity for visual enjoyment.

Xato Sauce

¼ cup wine vinegar
½ cup olive oil
1 teaspoon cayenne pepper
3 cloves garlic
1 teaspoon salt
10 toasted almonds

257

Spain

1. As the old vaudeville joke goes, first steal the toasted almonds from the gal who's making them to serve with cocktails. If this is inconvenient or contrary to principle, toast them according to the directions on page 254 but you can omit the oil and salt.
2. Blend all ingredients in a blender at high speed until smooth.

VEGETABLE CASSEROLE

3 *lbs potatoes*
3 *cups onions, sliced*
6 *tomatoes*
1 *lb can whole string beans*
1 *teaspoon pepper*
1 *tablespoon salt*
6 *tablespoons butter*
  olive oil

1. Heat oven to 400°.
2. Peel the potatoes and cut each one into 6 pieces. Cut the tomatoes into 6 or 8 pieces, depending on the size.
3. Rub the bottom and sides of a casserole with olive oil. Put all ingredients into the casserole except the butter.
4. Dot the surface with bits of butter.
5. Bake for 50 minutes, uncovered, stirring 2 or 3 times in the course of the baking.

> Note: You can prepare the casserole in advance and reheat before serving. On the other hand, the hostess' oven won't be in use for this dinner and it might be better to prepare the casserole for

baking and then pop it into the oven at cocktail time.

SWEET BREAD

> *4 eggs*
> *½ lb salted butter, softened to room temperature*
> *2 and ½ cups sugar, sifted*
> *3 and ½ cups flour, sifted*
> *2 tablespoons baking powder*
> *¼ teaspoon saffron*
> *¾ cup milk*
> *2 tablespoons brown sugar*
> *¾ cup currants*
> *¾ cup peanuts, chopped coarsely*
> *½ teaspoon cloves mixed with 1 teaspoon sugar*

1. Separate the eggs, putting the whites in a small mixer bowl.
2. In large bowl of electric mixer, cream the butter and sugar together. Add egg yolks and mix well.
3. Sift the flour, baking powder and saffron powder together.
4. Add the flour mixture and the milk alternately, about a quarter at a time, mixing well after each addition.
5. Clean the beaters of the mixer and, in the small mixer bowl, beat the egg whites to the soft peak stage. Fold into the batter.
6. Divide the batter into two loaf pans. Heat the oven to 350°.

7. Sprinkle the brown sugar, currants and peanuts over the top of the loaves. (If they've disappeared when the loaves are removed from the oven, don't worry; they've sunk down into the batter and you'll find them again.)
8. Rub the clove and sugar mixture with the back of a spoon and sprinkle the mixture over the breads.
9. Let the breads stand at room temperature for 10 minutes before baking.
10. Bake for 45 minutes.

NATILLA

   5 *cups milk*
       grated rind of 1 and ½ lemons
   1 *cinnamon stick*
  ½ *teaspoon salt*
   1 *and ½ cups sugar*
   7 *eggs*
   1 *and ½ teaspoons vanilla*
   2 *and ½ tablespoons cornstarch*
  ¼ *cup cold water*
       cinnamon

1. Put the milk, lemon rind, cinnamon stick and salt in a saucepan and bring to the boiling point. Remove from heat and let cool for 10 minutes.
2. Mix the sugar, eggs and vanilla together. When the milk has cooled, remove the cinnamon stick and pour the milk gradually into the egg mixture, stirring constantly.

3. Mix the cornstarch with the cold water thoroughly and stir the mixture into the custard.
4. Cook over low heat, stirring, until the mixture thickens. Keep the heat low since you don't want it to boil.
5. Pour the custard into a serving bowl, sprinkle it lightly with cinnamon and refrigerate.

JAPAN

MENU

Sake

Pickled Clams

Bean Soup

Teriyaki

Cucumber Ring Garnish

Zucchini

Pickled Eggplant with Mustard

Sweet Bean Cakes

Jasmine Tea

When I was young and growing up in New York (and we'll have no questions from the balcony on the subject of Washington's Farewell Address to his troops) I don't remember a single Japanese restaurant in mid-Manhattan. As a matter of fact, I think the first time I was ever in a Japanese restaurant was with my brother, Harvey, (another honored Eat-In member) when he returned from a tour of duty as a naval officer in Japan where he acquired a taste for Japanese food. Between similarly intrigued servicemen and the businessmen who have been introduced to the cuisine by way of the sumptuous banquets which seem to be the **sine qua non** of doing business in Japan, the enthusiasm for Japanese cooking has spread to the point where New York and other cities now boast an excellent selection of Japanese restaurants. And all of us to whom it is applicable have now learned the hard way the cardinal rule about eating in Japanese restaurants where one sits cross-legged on the floor: NEVER wear a girdle. Paralysis will set in and it's humiliating to be hauled back onto your feet by some lithe waitress who has been doing deep knee bends without visible effort every time she serves a dish.

Japanese cooking, like Chinese, tends to use a large proportion of vegetables and rice or noodles to a small proportion of meat. Food is served in small pieces and eaten with chopsticks. The soybean and its derivatives—sauce, bean curd, sprouts, etc.—are equally important in both cuisines. Unlike the Chinese, however, Japanese use potatoes extensively and the use of meat is a relatively modern adoption. Because of the Buddhist influence, meat was not popular in Japan (except among foreigners) until the middle of the nineteenth century. An American diplomat is credited with

264

having introduced beef into Japan, but it did not become accepted until some fifteen years later when the emperor tried it, liked it and, of course, was rapidly imitated by the "In Crowd" of his day. Following the fashion must have been difficult in this case since Orientals did not like the smell of milk or butter or meat and claimed that butter-eaters and meat-eaters acquired an offensive personal odor as a result of their dietary habits.

For a people who acquired the meat habit late in their history, it is interesting that the Japanese produce what many experts consider to be the finest beef in the world. The legendary best of the Kobe beef comes from cattle which are hand raised, fed beer by the bottle and hand massaged daily with sake to spread the fat evenly through-out the meat. (Before you start nagging your butcher for this kind, I hasten to report that it never gets far from the area in which it is raised and you'll probably have to make a trip to Japan to try it.)

For a traditional Japanese dinner, no large serving dishes are ever placed on the table. Individual servings are placed before each diner on trays, either at individual small tables or at a large table for less formal dining. While you're prob-ably not equipped to run your dinner this way, you might try adopting some of the easier pleasant Japanese customs— like providing the guests with o-shibori instead of napkins. These are the warm, wet towels brought and taken away immediately after use at intervals throughout the meal. And if one of you is clever with her hands, the beautiful vege-table garnishes which make Japanese food so attractive would be a nice addition. Radish or turnip flowers or thinly sliced carrots pared into petal or star shapes are a nice insert for the hors d'oeuvres or the main course. If that seems too ambitious, the cucumber garnish suggested for the teriyaki is simple enough even for the fainthearted or fumble-fingered.

Bread is not indigenous to Japanese cuisine. The wheat grown in Japan is more suited to making noodles, and bread has only begun to be fairly popular in the last twenty-five years since American wheat has been imported. This leaves your bread-and-wine contributor with nothing to do—a problem which we solved happily by having both an hors d'oeuvre and soup.

SHOPPING SOURCES

Mail order Japanese food sources are hard to come by. Luckily there are substitutes which can be used if there is no Japanese food store in your area or if it is inconvenient to use one of those listed below.

Most good wine and liquor dealers carry sake. Mirin is less commonly stocked. If you can't find it, you can substitute sherry, adding about one third as much sugar as sherry, mixing the sugar into the sherry before using it.

We do suggest you go a bit out of your way if necessary to get Japanese tea—either the jasmine we used or green tea. The teas are very delicate and compliment the food well.

While Kikkoman soy sauce is generally available and very good, if you are ordering from either Katagiri & Co., Inc. or The Japan Mart, Inc., you might want to experiment with other Japanese soy sauces which you will find listed as "shoyu."

For sources of fresh ginger, see p. 152-3.

AMERICAN TEA, COFFEE AND SPICE CO., 1511 Champa St., Denver, Colorado 80202. Catalogue available. (azuki beans and an excellent selection of Japanese teas)

THE JAPAN MART INC., 239 West 105 Street, New York, N. Y. 10025. Catalogue available. (azuki beans, miso, shoyu, Japanese teas)

KATAGIRI & CO., INC., 224 East 59th Street, New York, N. Y. 10022. Catalogue available. (azuki beans, miso, shoyu, Japanese teas)

ORIENTAL FOOD SHOP, 1302 Amsterdam Avenue, New York, N. Y. 10027. Catalogue available. (Jasmine tea)

PAPRIKAS WEISS, 1546 Second Avenue, New York, N. Y. 10028. Catalogue 25¢. (Jasmine and green tea)

Japan

SAKE

Sake, a light rice wine, is served warm in small china cups. The appropriate little porcelain bottle and cups are pretty and not expensive if you have access to a Japanese shop. If not, use any fairly small glass or china container and warm the sake by placing the container in a pan of hot water for 5-10 minutes before serving. Have another container warming while the first is being consumed so that a fresh supply of warm wine is available throughout the meal.

You can, if you like, try a sake martini by shaking equal amounts of sake and gin with cracked ice and straining the martini into the glass. We opt for straight warm sake.

PICKLED CLAMS

3 dozen cherrystone clams, shelled
¼ cup white wine vinegar
¼ cup soy sauce
½ cup sake
½ cup sugar

1. Combine all ingredients except clams. Mix well.
2. Pour the mixture over the clams and refrigerate overnight.
3. Serve, speared with toothpicks, with cocktails.

BEAN SOUP

Miso is a mashed fermented soybean paste frequently used as the basis for Japanese soups. If you have trouble finding it, you can make an acceptable substitute by using your blender to purée 2 and ¼ cups of drained canned chick peas and then adding 3 tablespoons of vinegar and 3 tablespoons of beer to the mixture. Remove the mixture to a bowl and let it stand at room temperature while you do the rest of the preparation of the soup.

> 10 oz miso (or substitute described above)
> 8 cups beef broth
> ¾ cup turnips, grated
> 1 and ½ cups carrots, grated
> ½ lb raw shrimp
> 6 eggs, beaten
> ¼ cup soy sauce
> ½ cup chopped scallions

1. If grating carrots and turnips frays your knuckles and your patience, do the job the easy way by cutting the carrots into small chunks and placing them in the blender with a little of the beef broth. Strain the liquid back into the cooking pot before measuring the grated carrots. Repeat the same procedure with chunks of turnip.
2. Shell, devein and chop the shrimp into small pieces.
3. Put the beef broth in a large pot and bring to a boil. Add the shrimp, carrots and turnips and simmer for 10 minutes.
4. Add some of the hot broth to the miso or bean mixture and stir, then add the mixture to the pot of soup, stir and let simmer for 5 minutes.

269

5. Mix the beaten eggs, soy sauce and scallions together. If the soup is to be eaten immediately, stir the mixture into the soup and cook, stirring for 1 minute before removing from the heat. If the soup is to be transported, carry the egg mixture in a separate jar and add it at the last minute after the soup has been reheated.

TERIYAKI

4½–5 lbs boneless sirloin steak
½ cup soy sauce
¼ cup mirin (or ¼ cup sherry mixed with 1 tablespoon sugar)
¼ cup sake
¼ cup sugar
1 tablespoon rice wine
4 cloves garlic, minced
¼ cup freshly ground ginger
2 tablespoons oil
¼ teaspoon salt

1. Combine all ingredients except the steak in a glass or china bowl and mix well.
2. Marinate the steak in the mixture for 4 hours, turning frequently.
3. Remove the steak from the marinade but reserve the marinade for both basting and serving.
4. Broil the steak, basting with the marinade occasionally.
5. Slice the steak. Strain the marinade and pour it over the steak slices before serving.

CUCUMBER RING GARNISH

2 cucumbers

1. Wash the cucumbers well. Run the tines of a fork along the skin from top to bottom on all sides to score.
2. Cut off and discard the rounded ends and cut each cucumber into ¼ inch slices. With a sharp knife, remove the center of each slice, leaving only the rind and about ¼ inch of cucumber around the edges.
3. Make a cut through the rim of each of half the cucumber slices. Slip an uncut cucumber slice through the cut to link the 2 slices.

ZUCCHINI

A wok is the ideal utensil for making this dish. If none is available, a heavy cast-iron pot with a tight fitting cover is the best substitute.

3 lbs zucchini
5 large cloves garlic, minced
¼ cup peanut oil
salt and pepper

1. Wash zucchini but do not peel it. Cut into ½ inch diagonal slices.

271

2. Heat the peanut oil **very slowly** over a low flame; half an hour is not too much. After 15 minutes, add the minced garlic.
3. Add the zucchini. Cook and stir for 5 minutes. Cover the wok or pot and continue cooking over same low flame for 5 minutes more.
4. Turn heat to medium, remove the cover and cook, stirring for 5 minutes.
5. Remove zucchini with a slotted spoon, sprinkle with salt and pepper and serve.

PICKLED EGGPLANT WITH MUSTARD

> 2 *medium eggplants*
> *salt*
> 1 *tablespoon dry mustard*
> 1 *and ¼ tablespoons water*
> ¾ *cup soy sauce*
> 5 *tablespoons sugar*
> ¼ *cup white wine vinegar or rice wine vinegar*

1. Peel eggplants and slice crosswise in ¼ inch slices.
2. Sprinkle the eggplant slices with salt and let them stand at room temperature for 1 hour. Drain off the liquid.
3. Make a paste of the mustard and water and then add the rest of the ingredients. Mix.
4. Pat the eggplant slices dry and cut each slice in quarters. Place in bowl and add sauce, turning the slices in the sauce several times.
5. Refrigerate for 1 hour before serving.

SWEET BEAN CAKES

You can make the pastry dough the night before you plan to bake the cakes or you can prepare it while the beans are cooking. If you plan to make the dough earlier, start at Step 6.

Don't hesitate to use lima beans if it's inconvenient to get the Azuki beans; the Japanese friend who gave Marion the recipe uses them as a matter of preference.

4 cups flour, sifted
4 teaspoons baking powder
2 cups sugar
½ cup butter
3 large eggs
1 teaspoon salt
1 cup Azuki red beans or dried lima beans

1. If using red beans, soak them overnight, then drain and proceed with following preparation for either type of beans.
2. Place the beans in a pot and cover with water about an inch and a half over the top of the beans. Bring to a boil, reduce heat and simmer until the beans are soft and the skins slip off easily—about 2 and ½ hours.
3. Place the beans in a colander and press with a wooden spoon to force the beans through and leave the hulls behind. Catch the beans in a clean towel placed below the colander. Gather up the ends of the towel and squeeze hard to drain off any excess liquid.
4. Place the beans in a pan and add the salt and 1 cup of the sugar. Cook, stirring until all the sugar is dis-

273

solved and the mixture is about the consistency of cold mashed potatoes.

5. Cool the bean mixture and shape into about 20 marble shaped balls.
6. To make the pastry, cream the butter and 1 cup of the sugar. Add 2 eggs and the white of the third, one egg at a time, mixing well after each addition. (Reserve the yolk of the third egg for brushing the pastry.)
7. Sift the flour and baking powder into the butter-egg mixture and blend.
8. Turn the pastry onto a lightly floured board and shape the dough into 3 rolls about 1 and ½ inches in diameter. The dough can either be used immediately or wrapped tightly in waxed paper and stored in the refrigerator for several days.
9. When you are ready to bake, cut the pastry rolls into slices about ¾ inch thick. Make a slight depression in the center of each slice and place a bean paste ball in the depression. Fold the dough over the bean paste and pat the pastry into a football shape, with the pinched edges on the bottom.
10. Place the cakes on a Teflon or lightly buttered cookie sheet and brush the tops with the reserved beaten egg yolk.
11. Bake at 400° for 15-20 minutes.

CARIBBEAN

MENU

Planter's Punch

Lobster Vinaigrette

Sherried Chicken

Okra Stew

Pineapple Salad

Caribbean Cornsticks

Banana Cake

I'm always fascinated by the culinary prejudices of a cannibalistic society. In some islands of the Caribbean where cannibalism was prevalent not too many centuries ago, there was, we are assured, a decided preference for Frenchmen who were reputedly of delicate flavor while Spaniards were tough and stringy to the gourmet palate.

I hasten to assure you that you won't have occasion to test the theory (or be tested by it) today on any island you happen to be lucky enough to visit. Pork is the favored meat with chicken following a close second, and, of course, the wealth of fish which graces any island cooking. There are differences in the cuisines of the various islands as a result of the fact that some of them were settled by the French and others by the Spanish, the English, the Dutch and the Danes and, more recently, by people from the United States. Each has left its mark on the cuisine of particular islands. So, too, did the African slaves and the Oriental and Indian laborers who came in the nineteenth century after the abolition of slavery. What the islands have in common largely revolves around the fruits and vegetables, many of which, unfortunately, you're not likely to be able to find at home unless you live in a city with a substantial Puerto Rican or Cuban population—guava, mango, papaya, breadfruit, plantain. You won't have trouble finding the islands' great fruit contribution—pineapple —which originated here, not in Hawaii as most people believe. (If you want a small architectural note as a bonus, the popularity of the pineapple in both American and European design as a decoration for gateposts or doors originated in the fact that it was a Caribbean sign of hospitality to have a pineapple on the door of a hut.)

Black beans and rice are another element so common to island cooking that it seems almost illegal to have omitted them from our menu. They were left out because an excellent version of the dish is part of the Brazilian dinner.

There are those who will argue that the islands' most important contribution to the stomach of the world was the rum which originated as a by-product of sugar cane production. Its popularity spread during the seventeenth century when the British Navy started serving rum to sailors instead of the traditional beer, which had an unpleasant tendency to go sour after a few weeks at sea. I can give personal testimony to the miraculous powers of Caribbean rum; it can enable you to ride a tandem bicycle. Several years ago while attending a meeting in Puerto Rico, a number of us decided late one afternoon to rent bicycles. Nothing was left but tandems and I, who am celebrated for my lack of coordination, found myself riding behind a large gentleman who was my equal in ineptitude but whose size effectively blocked out the horizon. After half an hour of sheer terror in which I found myself wondering why I had thought **flight** insurance was necessary for this trip, we stopped for a long cool drink (or two) of pineapple and rum. I don't know what the bystanders were staring at during our ride back, since, as far as we were concerned, we had mastered the tandem thoroughly and were riding with unbelievably effortless grace. (This isn't the way our hysterical colleagues described it.) Small wonder that the British Navy, similarly fortified, racked up its superb record.

If you're driving home, however, have the Planters Punch at the beginning of the meal and end it, if you can, with Jamaican Blue Mountain coffee, which many coffee buffs consider one of the great coffees of the world. If you can't find it locally, you can get it through one of the mail order houses listed below.

SHOPPING SOURCES

ANTONE'S, P. O. Box 3352, Houston, Texas 77001. Catalogue available.

MARYLAND GOURMET MART, 414 Amsterdam Avenue, New York, N. Y. 10024. Catalogue available.

Caribbean

PLANTER'S PUNCH

You can work up an argument between Planter's Punch aficionados on the delicate question of whether club soda does or does not belong in it. We chose the peaceful way; fill each glass about half full of the punch without soda, serve the club soda on the side and let each expert go his own merry way.

2–3 thinly sliced limes
1 quart dark rum
2 and ½ cups fresh lime juice
1 and ½ cups confectioner's sugar
½ teaspoon Angostura bitters
crushed ice
club soda

1. Make a cut in each lime slice from the outer edge to the center of the slice. Put a slice of lime on the rim of each glass by sliding the slit over the rim.
2. Mix the rum, lime juice, sugar and bitters in your largest pitcher until the sugar is thoroughly dissolved.
3. Fill each glass about half full of crushed ice and pour the punch over the ice, leaving a little room to add club soda for those who want to do so.

LOBSTER VINAIGRETTE

> *1 and ½ lbs lobster meat*
> *¾ cup olive oil*
> *½ cup tarragon vinegar*
> *1 and ½ teaspoons salt*
> *3 medium onions, sliced*
> *1 green pepper, chopped*
> *2 tablespoons parsley, minced*
> *lettuce leaves*

1. Put lobster in a saucepan with enough water to cover. Bring to a boil, reduce heat and simmer for 4 minutes. Drain.
2. When lobster is cool enough to handle, cut it into small pieces.
3. Combine all other ingredients except the lettuce leaves and mix well.
4. Pour sauce over lobster and refrigerate for at least 4 hours.
5. Serve on lettuce leaves.

SHERRIED CHICKEN

> *6 chicken breasts, split*
> *¾ cup sherry*
> *¾ cup butter*
> *1 large can tomatoes (2 lb, 3 oz)*
> *1 and ½ lbs small white onions*
> *1 and ½ tablespoons salt*
> *2 bay leaves*
> *¾ cup pimento stuffed olives*

Caribbean

The Night Before

1. Rinse chicken and pat dry with paper towels.
2. Put chicken in a glass or china bowl, cover with sherry and refrigerate overnight.

The Day of the Dinner

1. Remove chicken from sherry. Reserve sherry.
2. Melt half the butter in a Dutch oven or large casserole. Brown the chicken pieces about 5 minutes on each side.
3. Add the sherry and all remaining ingredients except the olives.
4. Cover pot and simmer for 1 hour.
5. Add the olives and cook, uncovered, for 1 hour more.

OKRA STEW

1 and ½ lbs fresh okra
2 tablespoons oil
¼ lb slice of ham
1 large onion, chopped
1 green pepper, chopped
2 sweet potatoes
¼ cup tomato sauce
1 tablespoon salt
¼ teaspoon red pepper flakes
4 cups water

1. Cut tips off okra pods and cut in ½ inch slices. Rinse thoroughly under running cold water.
2. Chop onions and green pepper. Peel sweet potatoes and cut in cubes to make 1 and ½ cups of potato cubes.
3. Dice ham into small cubes.
4. Heat oil in saucepan. Add ham cubes and cook for about 3 minutes until ham is slightly browned.
5. Add all other ingredients. Bring to a boil.
6. Reduce heat and simmer, covered, for 30 minutes. Remove cover and continue to cook for another 10 minutes.

PINEAPPLE SALAD

You can use drained canned pineapple chunks if this dinner comes at a time of year when fresh pineapple is not available. The fresh fruit makes a better salad.

>   *1 or 2 fresh pineapples (depending on size)*
>   *small bunch watercress*
> *½ cup olive oil*
> *2 tablespoons lime juice*
> *1 tablespoon vinegar*
> *½ teaspoon salt*

1. Peel pineapple and cut in slices. Then cut each slice into cubes.
2. Wash and chop watercress.
3. Combine all other ingredients and mix well.
4. Just before serving, pour dressing over pineapple cubes and decorate with watercress.

Caribbean

CARIBBEAN CORNSTICKS

These tasty little fried rolls show up in various countries of the Caribbean under slightly different names, sometimes round instead of oblong, sometimes with grated Parmesan or Edam or Gouda rather than the cheddar we used. In any version, we think you'll like them.

3 cups water
1 tablespoon salt
1 and ½ cups yellow cornmeal
1 cup mild cheddar cheese, grated
1 and ½ cups vegetable oil for frying

1. Combine water and salt in a heavy saucepan. Bring to a boil. Pour the cornmeal in so gradually that the water never stops boiling, stirring constantly as you add the cornmeal.
2. Cook for about 3 minutes after the last of the cornmeal has been added, stirring.
3. Remove the pot from the stove and stir in the cheese. Let the mixture cool to room temperature.
4. Wet your hands with cold water and shape the rolls into cylinders about the length of your middle finger and about an inch wide. (You should have about 20 little rolls.)
5. The rolls should be allowed to stand at room temperature for at least an hour before they are fried. If, however, there is going to be a long delay, they can be refrigerated, covered with plastic wrap, for several hours.
6. When you start to cook the rolls, line a cookie sheet with paper towels and put it in a 250° oven to hold the warm rolls as you finish them.

284

7. In a skillet, heat the oil until it is very hot (400° if you're using an electric pan) and fry the rolls, 4 or 5 at a time, turning as they brown. They will take about 4-5 minutes altogether. Put the finished rolls in the oven while you do the rest.

Note: The rolls can be made ahead of time and re-heated in the oven just before serving. They're a little better the other way; since nobody else will be frying in the kitchen for this meal, you may find it convenient for the breadmaker to take her drink into the kitchen and polish these off during cocktail time.

BANANA CAKE

½ cup sweet butter, softened to room temperature
1 tablespoon lemon rind, grated
1 cup sugar
1 teaspoon vanilla extract
2 eggs
2 cups flour, sifted
1 teaspoon baking powder
½ teaspoon salt
2 ripe bananas
¼ cup milk

1. Put butter, lemon rind, sugar and vanilla in large bowl of electric mixer. Beat until light and fluffy. Add eggs, one at a time, beating after each addition.

285

Caribbean

2. Sift flour, baking powder and salt into another bowl. In still another bowl, mash the bananas with the milk.
3. Add the flour and the mashed banana alternately to the mixing bowl, adding about ⅓ of each at a time and beating after each addition.
4. Pour cake mixture into 2 cake pans. Bake at 375° for 25 minutes.
5. Turn layers out on a rack to cool before frosting.

Banana Icing

> ½ *cup butter, softened to room temperature*
> 3 *cups confectioners' sugar*
> ½ *teaspoon salt*
> 2 *ripe bananas, mashed*
> 1 *tablespoon rum*

1. In bowl of electric mixer, beat the sugar, salt and butter until smooth.
2. Add remaining ingredients and beat again.
3. Frost tops and sides of layers.

SWITZERLAND

MENU

Cocktails

Quiche Monique

Mehlsuppe

Stuffed Breast of Veal

Green Bean Salad

Swiss Braided Bread

Chocolate Fondue

1969 NEUFCHATEL CHATEAU DE BEAUREGARD

Switzerland is a land of four languages and four cuisines—French, German, Italian and Swiss. Listening to a Swiss waiter switch blithely from one language to another may make you shrink back into your chair in the hope of having your unilingual status undiscovered. But it's worth perking up long enough to order in any language—you'll love the combination of food styles.

Aside from the three prime influences in the various sections of Switzerland, there are indigenous Swiss specialties which you will find in all areas—cheese in all shapes, manners and forms and the prevalent use of ice cream as dessert. It is the only country I know where the dessert menu of elegant restaurants reads like a Howard Johnson sundae list. It may be a novelty to top off a gourmet dinner with a banana split but don't knock it till you've tried it, using rich Swiss ice cream which leads to the instantaneous decision to worry about your weight on your own home cooking.

Cheese turns up as hors d'oeuvre, in the cooking of soups and main courses, in salads, as dessert and, of course in the famous Swiss fondue, which consists of cheese, wine and seasoning heated in a fondue pot into which each diner dunks chunks of bread on a long fork. The fondue is an excellent example of necessity sometimes being the mother of fabulous cooking inventions. Bread and cheese were the chief available foods. Cheese was made in the summer and fall and hardened. What do you do with hard cheese and hard bread? If you're the ingenious Swiss, you invent the fondue.

My own favorite cheese dish of Switzerland is raclette, which many traveling Americans seem to miss entirely unless they've been alerted to look for it. Raclette is made by putting a semisoft cheese in front of a fire or a vertical charcoal brazer, scraping off the meltings and serving them over small hot new potatoes. Well worth tracking down when you're in Switzerland.

Our menu reflected some of the French and some of the German influence on Swiss cuisine and, I must confess, a bit of American. The chocolate fondue is reputed to have been invented by the chef of a Swiss restaurant in New York. I can't understand why the Swiss didn't think of it first since it combines their fondue concept with Swiss chocolate which is great enough to puff the Swiss chest with pride. (We'll overlook for the moment the problems of how much of it can be consumed without puffing a chocoholic in other places.) While I haven't encountered the chocolate fondue in Switzerland myself, I am told that it has caught on in places there too.

You can, if you like, adapt the old Swiss fondue custom to the chocolate fondue. This requires that any lady who drops her fondue off her fork has to kiss the gentleman sitting next to her and any gentleman who drops his must pay for the next bottle of wine. If the latter penalty seems inappropriate for dinner at home, you might try making the penalty washing the dishes for one course.

SHOPPING SOURCES

If you have trouble finding Swiss chocolate in your area, you can order it from:

ANTONE'S, P. O. Box 3352, Houston, Texas
77001. Catalogue available.

PAPRIKAS WEISS, 1546 Second Avenue, New
York, N. Y. 10028. Catalogue 25¢.

H. ROTH & SON, 1577 First Avenue, New York,
N. Y. 10028 or 968 Second Avenue, New York, N. Y.
10022. Catalogue available. (An unusually fine selection of Tobler chocolate bars)

If you have already discovered and enjoyed raclette or
have ambition to try it, Cheeses of All Nations, 153
Chambers Street, New York, N. Y. 10007, has the hard-
to-find Valais cheese and will ship it. If you don't have an
open fireplace, the same shop sells a Swiss Raclette stove
or will rent you one if you happen to live in the New
York area. Catalogue available.

Switzerland

QUICHE MONIQUE

We've named this quiche in honor of Monique Eastman because she taught Elizabeth and me the secret of pastry in one revelatory Saturday afternoon. This is quite a tribute to her teaching, considering that up to that time neither of us had been able to produce a pastry crust that was distinguishable from our children's Play-Do. This versatile dough can be used not only for a quiche, but for tarts, fruit pies or filled hors d'oeuvres that can be frozen and baked as the need arises. If there are any scraps left over, reroll them about ¼ inch thick, cut into rounds with a juice glass, sprinkle with sugar and cinnamon and bake at 350° until nicely browned—about half an hour—and you'll have delicate, delicious cookies.

The following recipe makes enough dough to line an 11 and ½ inch tart pan.

Pastry

> ½ *lb cream cheese*
> ½ *lb sweet butter*
> 1 *teaspoon salt*
> 2 *cups flour*

1. Let the butter and cream cheese stand at room temperature until very soft. Place in the large bowl of your electric mixer and beat, first at medium speed and then at high speed until the mixture is smooth. Put the mixer at low speed and add the salt and then the flour gradually.
2. Remove the mixture from the bowl and form into a ball.

292

Wrap it in waxed paper and refrigerate the dough for four hours. (It can be left in the refrigerator overnight, if you wish, but if it is, let the dough stand at room temperature for half an hour before rolling it.)

3. Place the dough on a lightly floured board and have a small saucer of flour at hand. With the rolling pin, flatten the top of the ball of dough very gently, always moving your rolling pin from the center to the edge, with a little more pressure on the pin at the center of the pastry and less pressure near the edge. Turn the ball frequently, continuing to work from the center to the outside and sprinkling the top with a light dusting of flour from time to time. You'll find this produces a kind of flap around the edges. Put down the rolling pin and pat the sides down from time to time. Continue to turn the dough until it has become sufficiently large and flat to make turning unwieldy. Roll the dough by this method into a 13-inch circle.

4. Roll one end of the circle over your rolling pin and then turn the pin so that the whole pastry circle is rolled around the rolling pin. Unroll it over the tart pan. With your fingers, ease the dough into the sides of the pan. Run the rolling pin firmly over the top of the pan and the excess dough will fall away. With a fork, prick the bottom crust in a dozen places. The crust can be used immediately or refrigerated until needed.

The Filling

2 cups heavy sweet cream
8 eggs
6 slices of ham, diced
6 slices of cooked bacon, diced
6 oz Swiss cheese

293

Switzerland

1. Grate the Swiss cheese. Your blender will do the job well.
2. Mix all ingredients.

To Bake the Quiche

1. Heat the oven to 375°.
2. Put the tart shell in the oven for 5 minutes; then remove it and pour the filling into the shell.
3. Bake for 1 hour and serve immediately.

MEHLSUPPE

Don't be fooled by the fact that the list of ingredients doesn't look particularly exciting. This is a delicious soup and well worth its honored place in Swiss cooking.

> *1 and ½ sticks of sweet butter*
> *1 cup flour*
> *10 cups beef broth*
> *2 tablespoons caraway seeds*
> *2 cloves of garlic, crushed*
> *salt*
> *pepper*
> *1 cup milk*
> *grated Swiss cheese*

1. Melt the butter. Add the flour and cook over **very** low heat stirring constantly, until the flour is a golden brown.

(The trick is to get it really brown without burning. A low flame and patience will reward you with a richly colored soup.)

2. Add the broth gradually, stirring with a wire whisk.
3. Add the garlic, caraway seeds, salt and pepper and bring the mixture to a boil.
4. Reduce heat and simmer, covered, for 1 hour, stirring occasionally.
5. Just before serving, add the milk and simmer gently for 3 minutes, just until the soup is well heated; do not let it boil.
6. Pass the grated cheese as a garnish.

STUFFED BREAST OF VEAL

7 lb breast of veal
6 cups sliced apples
2 cups sliced onions
6 tablespoons butter
2 and ½ lbs sauerkraut
¼ cup gin
2 teaspoons salt
⅔ cup brown sugar
1 tablespoon caraway seeds
¾ cup oil

1. Have the butcher cut a deep pocket in the veal for stuffing.
2. Sauté the apples and onions in the butter over low heat until they turn a delicate brown.

295

3. Add all of the remaining ingredients except the veal and the oil. Cover and cook over low heat for 30 minutes, stirring occasionally.
4. Remove the cover, turn the heat high and cook until the liquid has evaporated.
5. Fill the veal pocket with the stuffing and close with string or skewers.
6. Brush the veal with oil and dust with salt and pepper.
7. Pour the remaining oil into a brown paper bag large enough to hold the roast. Holding the open end of the bag tightly closed, shake and turn the bag until the inside is well oiled.
8. Insert the roast, tie the open end of the bag shut and place it in a roasting pan.
9. Bake at 300° for 2 and ½ hours.

GREEN BEAN SALAD

2 *lbs fresh green beans*
2 *quarts boiling water*
1 *tablespoon sugar*
5 *tablespoons vinegar*
1 *large onion, finely chopped*
2 *teaspoons dried tarragon*
¼ *cup parsley, finely minced*
1 *teaspoon salt*
⅛ *teaspoon pepper*

1. Cut tips off string beans and drop them in the boiling water to which the sugar has been added.

2. Cook just until barely tender—about 10 minutes. Drain.
3. While the beans are cooking, mix all the remaining ingredients.
4. Put the drained beans in a large bowl and toss with the dressing mixture while the beans are still hot.
5. Let the dish stand at room temperature for 2 hours before serving. (You can refrigerate the dish if absolutely necessary but it's better if you can avoid chilling it.)

SWISS BRAIDED BREAD

1 package yeast
¼ cup warm water
1 stick sweet butter, softened to room temperature
2 tablespoons sugar
2 eggs, lightly beaten
2 teaspoons salt
1 cup scalded milk
5 cups flour
1 egg, beaten with 2 tablespoons heavy cream

1. Sprinkle the yeast over the warm water. Cover and let it stand in a warm place for about 7-8 minutes until it bubbles and expands.
2. Combine the butter, sugar, the 2 beaten eggs, salt and hot milk in a large mixing bowl.
3. When the milk mixture is lukewarm, add the yeast mixture and stir.
4. Add the flour gradually, stirring after each addition.

5. Turn the dough on to a lightly floured board and knead for 8 to 10 minutes.
6. Butter the sides and bottom of a large bowl and turn the dough in the bowl until all sides are lightly greased. Cover and let rise until it doubles in bulk.
7. Divide the dough into 8 equal parts and roll each part into a ball. Cover the dough balls with a towel and let them stand for 15 minutes while you butter a large cookie sheet.
8. Roll each ball into a long strip about 1 inch in diameter.
9. Place 4 of the strips on the cookie sheet, join them together at one end by folding under and tucking in and then braid the strips just as you would your daughter's hair. When the braiding is finished, join the strips at the other end.
10. Repeat with the remaining 4 strips for the second loaf.
11. Cover with a towel and let stand until they double in bulk again—about an hour.
12. Brush with the egg and cream mixture and bake at 375° for 35 minutes.

CHOCOLATE FONDUE

18 oz Swiss chocolate bars
1 cup light sweet cream
¼ cup Kirsch
sliced bananas
tangerine sections
whole strawberries
melon balls
pineapple chunks
sponge or pound cake, cut in small squares

1. Break the chocolate into small pieces in a fondue pot or chafing dish.
2. Add cream and Kirsch and cook over low heat, stirring, until chocolate is melted and mixture is hot.
3. Provide each guest with a fondue fork and an assortment of some or all of the goodies enumerated for dunking into the chocolate. If you're serving 10 people, a fondue pot or chafing dish for each end of the table is recommended.

INDEX

301

Index

Index

Index